THE AUSTRALIAN
Women's Weekly

Delicious
Gluten-free
FOOD

BAUER MEDIA GROUP

PUBLISHED IN 2016 BY BOUNTY BOOKS BASED ON MATERIALS LICENSED TO IT BY BAUER MEDIA BOOKS, AUSTRALIA.

BAUER MEDIA BOOKS ARE PUBLISHED BY
BAUER MEDIA PTY LIMITED
54 PARK ST, SYDNEY; GPO BOX 4088,
SYDNEY, NSW 2001 AUSTRALIA
PHONE +61 2 9282 8618; FAX +61 2 9126 3702
WWW.AWWCOOKBOOKS.COM.AU

PUBLISHER
JO RUNCIMAN

EDITORIAL & FOOD DIRECTOR
PAMELA CLARK

DIRECTOR OF SALES, MARKETING & RIGHTS
BRIAN CEARNES

CREATIVE DIRECTOR
HANNAH BLACKMORE

DESIGNER
JEANNEL CUNANAN

SENIOR EDITOR
STEPHANIE KISTNER

FOOD EDITOR
EMMA BRAZ

OPERATIONS MANAGER
DAVID SCOTTO

PRINTED IN CHINA
BY LEO PAPER PRODUCTS LTD

PUBLISHED AND DISTRIBUTED IN THE
UNITED KINGDOM BY BOUNTY BOOKS,
A DIVISION OF OCTOPUS PUBLISHING GROUP LTD
CARMELITE HOUSE
50 VICTORIA EMBANKMENT
LONDON, EC4Y 0DZ
UNITED KINGDOM
INFO@OCTOPUS-PUBLISHING.CO.UK;
WWW.OCTOPUSBOOKS.CO.UK

INTERNATIONAL FOREIGN LANGUAGE RIGHTS
BRIAN CEARNES, BAUER MEDIA BOOKS
BCEARNES@BAUER-MEDIA.COM.AU

A CATALOGUE RECORD FOR THIS BOOK IS
AVAILABLE FROM THE BRITISH LIBRARY.

ISBN: 978-0-7537-3108-6

© BAUER MEDIA PTY LTD 2016
ABN 18 053 273 546

THE AUSTRALIAN
Women's Weekly

Delicious
Gluten-free
FOOD

BB Bounty
Books

CONTENTS

Dr Joanna McMillan
Accredited Practising
Dietitian & Nutritionist
www.drjoanna.com.au

What is GLUTEN?

GLUTEN IS A TERM THAT INCLUDES A SELECTION OF *proteins* FOUND IN SOME GRAINS,

PRINCIPALLY *wheat* – INCLUDING THE INCREASINGLY POPULAR ANCIENT

WHEAT VARIETIES SPELT, KAMUT® KHORASAN WHEAT, EINKORN AND EMMER –

RYE, BARLEY AND TRITICALE (A CROSS BETWEEN WHEAT AND RYE).

THESE GRAINS MAKE *good bread* PRINCIPALLY BECAUSE OF GLUTEN.

IT ABSORBS WATER, GIVES *elasticity* TO THE DOUGH AND THE END RESULT IS A *chewier,*

LIGHTER TEXTURED BREAD. YOU'LL FIND THAT GLUTEN-FREE BREADS TEND TO BE *denser*

AND *tougher* AS A RESULT. IN MOST PEOPLE GLUTEN *does not cause* ANY PROBLEMS

AND IS DIGESTED ALONGSIDE ALL OTHER PROTEINS. HOWEVER, IN A GROWING NUMBER OF PEOPLE,

GLUTEN IS A PROBLEM AND GLUTEN-FREE DIETS HAVE INCREASED IN POPULARITY.

COELIAC DISEASE

Coeliac disease affects an estimated 1 in 70 Australians, although many of these don't know it, attributing their symptoms to general food intolerances or irritable bowel syndrome. But it's absolutely essential to get a proper diagnosis as there can be serious health consequences without the proper treatment – that is a lifelong, strictly gluten-free diet.

The gut is lined with millions of tiny hair-like projections called villi and microvilli. In the small intestine, where most nutrients are absorbed, these increase the surface area available for nutrient absorption by 60-120 times! In those with coeliac disease the immune system reacts abnormally to gluten, destroying these villi and microvilli, flattening the gut lining. This greatly reduces the surface area of the gut, causes inflammation and ultimately results in malnutrition.

Fortunately, the complete avoidance of gluten allows the gut lining to recover, prevents any further damage and the symptoms clear up. If you have had a diagnosis of coeliac disease, what is essential to know is that this is now a diet for life. The condition does not go away and so even minute amounts of gluten in your diet will cause damage.

This is why it is absolutely crucial to get a proper diagnosis. A strictly gluten-free diet is not as easy as it sounds – gluten itself or gluten-containing ingredients are frequently used in food products you might not expect including sauces and condiments, and although most cafes and restaurants have become savvier about catering for special diets, they may not always get it right. Hence you want to know how careful you need to be with avoiding all sources of gluten.

A word of warning; do not self-diagnose coeliac disease. If you cut out gluten from your diet and then see a doctor to try to gain a proper diagnosis, your gut will have healed and the biopsy used to confirm the condition will not show any damage. You need to have had gluten in your diet for the gastroenterologist to be able to make a correct diagnosis.

GLUTEN SENSITIVITY

In the absence of coeliac disease it is possible to have an intolerance to gluten. However, this is less easy to diagnose. As with all food intolerances the immune system is not involved and therefore allergy blood tests do not identify the problem food. It can only be done through trial and error, testing, eliminating and re-testing with the suspected foods.

The other problem is that often people try a gluten-free diet to treat gastrointestinal symptoms such as bloating, excessive gas, pain and discomfort. But these symptoms can

Gluten-containing FOODS

GRAIN

Varieties & products that may contain

Wheat

Bulgur, farro, freekeh, spelt, emmer, Kamut®, einkorn, durum wheat, bread, tortillas, wraps, breakfast cereals, croissants, pasta, couscous, noodles, pastries, semolina, farina, pies, doughnuts, biscuits, cake, banana bread, muffins, crumbed meat and fish, and sauces where wheat flour has been used to thicken e.g. béchamel sauce

RYE

Bread, pumpernickel bread, wraps, breakfast cereals, rye beer, crispbreads, crackers

Barley

Bread, wraps, breakfast cereals, malt extract, malt vinegar

TRITICALE

Biscuits, crispbreads, cakes, muffins & bread

* Note that wheat-free foods are not necessarily gluten-free and a wheat-free diet is not the same as a gluten-free diet. This is a common confusion. Some people have an intolerance to wheat, but are fine with other gluten-containing grains. This is another reason to ensure that you have a correct diagnosis to ensure you are following the optimal diet for you.

Gluten-free FOODS

ALL FRUITS

All vegetables,
including starchy vegetables such
as potatoes, sweet potatoes,
cassava and taro

**FRESH MEATS
(NOT CRUMBED)**

Nuts & seeds

**FISH & SEAFOOD
(NOT CRUMBED OR BATTERED)**

DAIRY FOODS

Fats & oils

RICE

**BUCKWHEAT & SOBA NOODLES
(MADE FROM 100% BUCKWHEAT)**

Millet

ARROWROOT

QUINOA

Amaranth

LEGUMES
dried beans,
chickpeas and lentils

TEFF

SORGHUM

Corn (maize)

TAPIOCA

GLUTEN-FREE FLOURS
besan (chickpea), nut flours such
as almond meal, lupin, green
banana, quinoa, amaranth, teff,
brown rice, potato, cornflour,
buckwheat and coconut

---

be due to a number of conditions and even if there is some improvement by cutting out gluten, the problem has not truly been identified. There is emerging evidence that for those people with irritable bowel syndrome (IBS) the real issue is with a number of fermentable short chain carbohydrates collectively known as FODMAPs. A low FODMAPs diet is appropriate in this situation and not a gluten-free diet.

The bottom line is that if you are having gut symptoms your doctor should be your first port of call to eliminate any medical cause and rule out or confirm coeliac disease. In the absence of any medical reason for your problems, then seeing an Accredited Practising Dietitian who specialises in food intolerances is your best way of identifying the problem and the most suitable diet for you.

If gluten sensitivity is suspected the good news is that you needn't be strictly gluten free – usually small levels of gluten can be tolerated. This makes the diet much easier to follow than the strictly gluten free diet for the treatment of coeliac disease.

WHAT ABOUT OATS?

Oats contain a slightly different protein and this has lead to controversy over whether they can in fact be included in a strictly gluten-free diet. One of the key problems is that oats are often harvested and processed in factories where gluten-containing grains are also processed. This can lead to cross-contamination. You will now find some oats in Australia labelled "wheat free" to indicate separate processing, or if imported from the USA or Europe they may say "gluten free".

However, the second problem is that even where there is no contamination with other grains, a small number of people with coeliac disease still have a problem with the proteins found in oats. Hence the current advice from Coeliac Australia is to avoid all oats unless under the supervision and testing of a medical practitioner.

For those of you following a gluten free or low gluten diet due to gluten sensitivity, you may well find that you can happily tolerate oats in your diet. This certainly broadens the variety in your diet and allows you to benefit from the fabulous nutrition of this grain. For the purposes of this book however we have not included oats in any of our recipes.

FOODS & DRINKS TO WATCH OUT FOR

SOUPS, SAUCES AND GRAVIES

since flour is a terrific thickener, soups, sauces and gravies often contain gluten. For cooking at home you can use cornflour or arrowroot to thicken instead of plain white flour and they work just as well. When buying ready-made however, be sure to check the labels carefully.

ALCOHOLIC DRINKS wine and distilled spirits are gluten free, however beers, ales and lagers made from gluten-containing grains (commonly barley) are not gluten free. With the rise in those following gluten-free diets there are now a number of gluten-free beers available in Australia and around the world. These are most commonly made from millet or sorghum and "gluten free" will be clearly indicated on the label.

OTHER DRINKS tea and coffee are gluten free, but do be careful with ready made powdered mixes as these may contain gluten. Similarly, while cocoa powder is gluten free, ready to mix drinking chocolate may not be. Drinks with malt extract or malt flavouring are made from barley and are not gluten free. Read the labels to be sure.

PACKAGED FOODS flour is often used in processing, even when you least expect it. For example, frozen chips may have wheat flour used to aid in creating a crispy coating, or a processed fruit bar may have flour used to help bind the product. If you need to be strictly gluten free, become an expert at reading food labels! Coeliac Australia has an endorsement program to aid with identifying gluten-free products. Look for the logo with a crossed grain. These products have been tested and contain no detectable gluten. There are also a number of Apps that can help you identify gluten-free products, even by simply scanning the barcode.

Tips FOR EATING OUT

Fortunately, more and more restaurants cater for all sorts of special diets and gluten free tends to be top of their list. This makes it much easier to eat out with confidence for those on gluten-free diets. Here are some tips to help:

★ ONLINE MENUS

Check out the restaurant menu online if possible before you go. If they don't have gluten-free options identified, call them to ask if they are able to cater for you. This is particularly important when dining with a larger group where there is a set menu. Most chefs will be willingly produce a gluten-free option if given notice.

★ INFORM AHEAD

Notifying the restaurant of any gluten-free diners in your group when you book is appreciated by most establishments.

★ TALK TO THE WAITER

On arrival at the restaurant make sure you talk to the waiter and politely explain that you have coeliac disease or a gluten intolerance and require a gluten-free diet. This helps to ensure they understand this is a genuine dietary restriction and not you just being a faddy eater!

★ DOUBLE CHECK

Use your knowledge of gluten-containing foods and ingredients to double check the menu gluten-free suggestions. Ask the waiter to confirm with the chef if there is anything you are worried about.

★ ASK THE CHEF

If when your food arrives you are not confident that it is in fact gluten free, question the staff and talk to the chef if necessary. Be polite and friendly so as to ensure the next customer requiring a gluten-free diet is catered for more easily.

Gluten-free Alternatives
TO TRADITIONAL GRAINS

QUINOA

Quinoa is cooked and eaten as a grain alternative, but it is in fact a seed. You'll often hear it called a pseudo-grain for that reason, similar to amaranth. While it might be relatively new to many of us, quinoa has been a staple food for thousands of years in the Andean region of South America. The Incas reportedly considered it sacred, calling it 'the mother of all grains'.

Nutritionally it has an impressive profile with double the protein of rice and unlike many grains, it contains all of the essential amino acids. It's also pretty fantastic for B group vitamins including folate and thiamin. Plus it has a low GI making it a pretty awesome gluten free option. Use anywhere you might have rice, toss through salads, make into a porridge or use the puffed grains in muesli. Quinoa flour can be used in baking.

Lupin Flour

LUPIN IS A LEGUME THAT IS GAINING ATTENTION FOR ITS POTENTIAL HEALTH BENEFITS. IT'S UNUSUAL IN THAT IT HAS A VERY LOW CARBOHYDRATE CONTENT, A HIGH CONTENT OF PROTEIN AND IS OUTSTANDING FOR FIBRE. NOT ONLY IS IT GLUTEN FREE, BUT WHEN YOU SUBSTITUTE SOME OF THE FLOUR IN A RECIPE FOR LUPIN FLOUR, YOU LOWER THE GLYCAEMIC INDEX AND THE GLYCAEMIC LOAD, HELPING YOU TO CONTROL YOUR BLOOD GLUCOSE LEVELS. SINCE GLUTEN-FREE FLOURS ARE OFTEN HIGH GI, THIS IS PARTICULARLY ADVANTAGEOUS WHEN COOKING GLUTEN FREE.

MILLET

Before rice was widely eaten in Asia, it is thought that different varieties of millet were the staple grain. Today millet is consumed all over the world, with India the largest producer and Nigeria coming in second.

Millet is almost always consumed as a whole grain and so delivers protein, fibre and B group vitamins. Millet has a mild flavour which pairs well with many foods and can be prepared to a produce a fluffy side dish similar to couscous or a creamy porridge. It's also fabulous cooked and added to salads.

To cook: add 2-2½ cups of water to 1 cup of millet and simmer for 20-30 minutes. Toasting millet before cooking helps to bring out the full flavour.

RICE

All rice is gluten free, but do look for wholegrain versions for the most nutrition. These contain more fibre than polished white rice and all of the nutrients are found in the outer husk of the grain. Brown rice is the most popular wholegrain variety, but look for wild rice, black rice and red rice for other options. You can use brown rice flour in baking and to thicken sauces.

Teff is a tiny grain that has been traditionally grown in Ethiopia and Eritrea. It's incredibly resilient and so thrives in the many difficult conditions of these areas of Africa. It is now gaining attention from the rest of the world due to its nutritional properties. It is high in a special type of fibre called resistant starch. This promotes the growth of beneficial bacteria in the gut, boosting immune function and promoting good gut health. It is also gluten free, and is especially high in calcium - terrific for those on dairy-free diets. It also has more iron, zinc and magnesium than wheat, with less phytic acid that reduces the absorption of these minerals. You can buy teff as the whole grain - these are tiny and sometimes called teff seeds - or as teff flour.

Buckwheat

BUCKWHEAT HAS BEEN A STAPLE FOOD FOR HUNDREDS OF YEARS IN ASIA AND EASTERN EUROPE. IT'S NOT RELATED TO WHEAT AT ALL, AND IS IN FACT RELATED TO RHUBARB AND SORREL. WHERE WHEAT IS A GRASS, BUCKWHEAT IS ACTUALLY A SEED, ALTHOUGH WE EAT IT AS A GRAIN. NUTRITIONALLY THE PROFILE IS MORE SIMILAR TO COMMON GRAINS, BUT LIKE QUINOA, IT CONTAINS ALL OF THE ESSENTIAL AMINO ACIDS. THIS MAKES IT A VALUABLE CHOICE FOR VEGETARIANS AND VEGANS. BUCKWHEAT IS USED IN JAPAN TO MAKE SOBA NOODLES. BUCKWHEAT ITSELF IS GLUTEN FREE, BUT IF YOU ARE STRICTLY GLUTEN FREE DO DOUBLE CHECK THE SOBA NOODLES YOU BUY ARE 100% BUCKWHEAT. THE JAPANESE BRANDS ARE USUALLY TRUE TO THIS, BUT SOMETIMES A COMBINATION OF BUCKWHEAT AND WHEAT FLOURS ARE USED.

AMARANTH

Amaranth is a pseudo-grain similar to quinoa. While it is less common today and may be new to you, it is an ancient grain and was a staple food of the Aztecs. Compared to other grains amaranth stands out for it's protein content – a cup of cooked amaranth has 9g compared to 5g in the same amount of brown rice. In addition to having good protein levels, amaranth has a good balance of amino acids – the building blocks of proteins. Most grains are low or lacking in lysine, but amaranth provides this essential amino acid. This makes it a particularly good choice for vegetarians and vegans.

Amaranth is an excellent source of the mineral manganese and is one of the grains with the most calcium, with 100g of uncooked amaranth providing 160mg – that's about 16% of the average adults daily requirement.

If you don't eat meat, including amaranth in your diet is a good way to boost your iron intake. A cup provides 5.2mg of iron. Bear in mind that plant iron – called non-haem iron – is very poorly absorbed but by including a good source of vitamin C in the same meal you can boost the absorption of the iron. Try adding cooked amaranth to your salad greens and sliced capsicum, both rich sources of vitamin C.

Breakfast

Poppy seed BAGELS

PREP + COOK TIME 50 MINUTES (+ STANDING) **MAKES** 10

- 3⅓ cups (450g) gluten-free plain (all-purpose) flour
- ½ cup (75g) potato flour
- ½ cup (90g) white rice flour
- ½ cup (75g) buckwheat flour
- 3 teaspoons (10g) dried yeast
- 2 teaspoons salt
- 2 teaspoons xanthan gum
- 1 egg
- 3 egg whites, reserve yolks
- ¾ cup (180ml) light olive oil
- 1½ cups (375ml) warm milk, plus 1 tablespoon extra
- 2 teaspoons poppy seeds
- 2 teaspoons flaked sea salt

TIPS

The longer you boil the bagels the chewer they become. Store bagels, wrapped in plastic wrap, in the fridge for up to 2 days or freeze for up to 3 months.

1 Combine sifted flours, yeast, salt and gum in a large bowl.

2 Place egg, egg whites, oil and milk in a large bowl of an electric mixer; beat on medium speed for 3½ minutes. Add the flour mixture, 1-cup at a time, beating until combined and smooth.

3 Turn dough onto a lightly floured surface and knead until smooth. Divide dough into 10 pieces. Roll each piece into a 24cm (9½-inch) long rope. Working with one length of dough at a time, shape into a ring until ends meet, securing ends together with a little water. Place rings on a greased oven tray. Repeat with remaining dough. Cover with oiled plastic wrap; stand in a warm place for 45 minutes.

4 Preheat oven to 200°C/400°F. Grease two oven trays then line with baking paper.

5 Working in batches of four, drop bagels one by one into a large saucepan of boiling water, ensuring they don't touch; boil for 1 minute. Turn bagels over; boil for another minute. Using a slotted spoon, transfer bagels to lined trays. Repeat with remaining bagels.

6 Brush tops of bagels with combined reserved egg yolks and extra milk; sprinkle with poppy seeds and sea salt. Bake for 25 minutes or until golden. Cool on a wire rack.

serving suggestion Serve lightly toasted, topped with smashed avocado, roasted cherry tomatoes, crumbled fetta and fresh oregano leaves, or simply spread with cream cheese or jam.

NUT FREE
GLUTEN FREE

**NUTRITIONAL
COUNT PER BAGEL
(BAGEL ONLY)**
21.8g total fat
4.5g saturated fat
1914kJ (458 cal)
54.9g carbohydrate
8.8g protein
0.7g fibre

Dairy free
GLUTEN FREE

**NUTRITIONAL
COUNT PER SERVING**
38.3g total fat
8.1g saturated fat
2250kJ (538 cal)
24.9g carbohydrate
13.8g protein
3.7g fibre

Chia pudding with coconut
& MACADAMIA CRUNCH

PREP + COOK TIME 15 MINUTES (+ REFRIGERATION) **SERVES** 4

- 3 cups (750ml) almond and coconut milk
- 1 cup (160g) white chia seeds
- 2 teaspoons vanilla bean paste
- ½ cup (55g) nibble mix
- ½ cup (70g) macadamia halves
- ⅓ cup (25g) shredded coconut
- 2 tablespoons dark agave nectar
- 125g (4 ounces) fresh raspberries

1 Combine milk, chia seeds and vanilla paste in a small bowl. Cover; refrigerate 4 hours or overnight.

2 Preheat oven to 180°C/350°F. Line an oven tray with baking paper.

3 Combine nibble mix, macadamias and coconut in a small bowl. Add agave; stir to combine. Sprinkle mixture on oven tray. Bake for 12 minutes or until toasted. Cool on tray. Break into small pieces.

4 Just before serving, spoon one-third of the chia mixture into four ¾ cup (180ml) serving glasses or jars; top with one-third of the nut mixture. Repeat layering, finishing with the nut mixture. Serve topped with raspberries.

TIPS

Chia puddings can be stored in the fridge for up to 4 days. Store nut crumble in an airtight container for up to 1 week. Swap raspberries for blueberries. Fresh figs would be delicious when in season.

Piña colada SMOOTHIE

PREP TIME 10 MINUTES SERVES 4 (MAKES 8 CUPS)

You will need about 1½ medium fresh pineapples, peeled and cored for the amount of pieces required.

- 1 cup (250ml) coconut water
- ⅔ cup (50g) desiccated coconut
- 900g (1¾ pounds) fresh pineapple pieces
- 30 ice cubes (375g)
- ¼ cup (60ml) lime juice

1 Blend coconut water, coconut and pineapple until well combined. Add ice and juice; blend until smooth.

2 Serve immediately topped with toasted coconut and lime slices, if you like.

TIPS

This smoothie is best made in a high-powered blender or nutribullet, vitamix or thermomix.

**NUTRITIONAL
COUNT PER SERVING**
8.7g total fat
6.7g saturated fat
814kJ (195 cal)
22.6g carbohydrate
2.3g protein
6g fibre

Dairy free
EGG FREE
GLUTEN FREE

**NUTRITIONAL
COUNT PER SERVING**
41g total fat
24g saturated fat
2052kJ (490 cal)
23.5g carbohydrate
4.9g protein
6.3g fibre

Papaya & macadamia salad
WITH COCONUT YOGHURT

PREP TIME 15 MINUTES **SERVES** 4

- 2 small papaya (1.3kg)
- 2 cups (560g) dairy-free coconut yoghurt
- ½ cup (70g) roasted macadamia halves
- ⅔ cup (30g) coconut flakes, toasted
- 1 tablespoon finely grated lime rind (see tips)
- 2 limes (180g), cut into wedges

1 Cut papaya in half lengthways; scoop out the seeds.

2 Spoon yoghurt into papaya hollow; sprinkle with macadamias, coconut and rind.

3 Serve immediately with lime wedges.

TIPS

If you have one, use a zester to cut the lime rind into long thin strips.

Sweet potato rösti with
SALMON & POACHED EGGS

PREP + COOK TIME 30 MINUTES **SERVES** 4

- 500g (1 pound) purple-skinned white-flesh sweet potato, peeled, grated coarsely
- 2 medium onions (300g), grated coarsely
- 2 egg whites
- ⅔ cup (50g) finely grated parmesan
- 2 tablespoons finely chopped fresh flat-leaf parsley
- 2 tablespoons finely chopped fresh dill
- 2 cloves garlic, crushed
- ⅓ cup (80ml) olive oil
- 40g (1½ ounces) butter
- 2 tablespoons white vinegar
- 8 eggs
- 300g (9½ ounces) hot-smoked salmon, flaked
- ½ cup (140g) greek-style yoghurt
- 1 tablespoon dukkah
- ⅓ cup fresh coriander (cilantro) leaves
- lemon wedges, to serve

1 Preheat oven to 180°C/350°F. Line an oven tray with baking paper.

2 Combine sweet potato and onion in a medium bowl; squeeze out excess liquid, return vegetables to bowl. Stir in egg white, parmesan, herbs and garlic; season.

3 Heat half the oil and half the butter in a large frying pan over medium heat. Spoon a quarter of the sweet potato mixture into pan, flatten to a 10cm (4-inch) round; cook for 3 minutes each side or until golden. Drain on paper towel; transfer to tray, season with salt. Repeat with remaining oil, butter and sweet potato mixture to make four rösti in total.

4 Bake rösti 10 minutes or until crisp and cooked through.

5 Meanwhile, to poach eggs, half-fill a large, deep-frying pan with water, add white vinegar; bring to a gentle simmer. Break 1 egg into a cup. Using a wooden spoon, make a whirlpool in the water; slide egg into whirlpool. Repeat with 3 more eggs. Cook eggs for 3 minutes or until whites are set and the yolks are runny. Remove eggs with a slotted spoon; drain on a paper-towel-lined plate. Repeat with remaining eggs.

6 Divide rösti between plates; top with salmon, eggs and yoghurt. Sprinkle with dukkah and coriander, serve with lemon wedges.

TIPS

Dukkah is a Middle Eastern nut and spice mixture available from supermarkets and delis. You can substitute kumara (orange sweet potato) or potato for the white sweet potato in the rösti and hot-smoked trout or white fish for the salmon.

**NUTRITIONAL
COUNT PER SERVING**
46g total fat
16g saturated fat
3055kJ (730 cal)
32g carbohydrate
44g protein
5g fibre

NUTRITIONAL COUNT PER SERVING
23.8g total fat
8.6g saturated fat
1957kJ (467 cal)
35g carbohydrate
25g protein
7.6g fibre

Dairy free
NUT FREE
GLUTEN FREE

Green quinoa
WITH SESAME EGGS

PREP + COOK TIME 25 MINUTES SERVES 4

- 1 cup (200g) white quinoa, rinsed
- 2 cups (500ml) gluten-free chicken or vegetable stock
- 8 eggs, at room temperature
- 1 tablespoon coconut oil
- 1 clove garlic, crushed
- 2 fresh small red chillis, chopped finely
- 4 cups (160g) thinly sliced kale (see tips)
- 4 cups (180g) firmly packed thinly sliced silver beet (see tips)
- 2 tablespoons lemon juice
- ½ cup finely chopped fresh flat-leaf parsley
- 2 tablespoons white sesame seeds
- 2 tablespoons black sesame seeds
- 1 teaspoon sea salt flakes

1 Place quinoa and stock in a medium saucepan; bring to the boil. Reduce heat to low-medium; simmer gently for 15 minutes or until most of the stock is absorbed. Remove from heat; cover, stand for 5 minutes.

2 Meanwhile, cook eggs in a small saucepan of boiling water for 5 minutes. Remove immediately from pan; cool under cold running water for 30 seconds. Peel.

3 Heat coconut oil in a medium saucepan over medium heat, add garlic and chilli; cook, stirring, for 2 minutes or until fragrant. Add kale and silver beet; stir until wilted. Stir in quinoa and juice; season to taste.

4 Combine parsley, sesame seeds and salt in a small bowl. Roll peeled eggs in sesame seed mixture.

5 Serve quinoa topped with eggs.

TIPS

You will need a bunch of kale and a bunch of silver beet for this recipe. Wash well before use.

Pancakes with grilled honey
BANANAS & RASPBERRIES

PREP + COOK TIME 20 MINUTES SERVES 4

- 1 cup (140g) sweet white sorghum flour
- ½ cup (70g) coconut flour
- 1 teaspoon baking powder
- ½ teaspoon bicarbonate of soda (baking soda)
- 2 eggs
- 1¾ cups (430ml) coconut milk
- 2 tablespoons dairy-free spread
- 4 medium bananas (800g), sliced thickly
- ¼ cup (90g) honey
- 125g (4 ounces) fresh raspberries

1 Combine dry ingredients in a medium bowl; make a well in the centre. Whisk in combined eggs and milk until batter is well combined (mixture will be thick).

2 Melt one-third of the dairy-free spread in a large non-stick frying pan over low-medium heat. Cooking four at a time, spoon 2 tablespoons of batter for each pancake into pan, flatten slightly; cook for 2 minutes or until lightly browned. Carefully turn over (mixture is delicate); cook for another 2 minutes or until cooked through. Remove from pan; keep warm. Repeat with remaining spread and batter to make 12 pancakes in total.

3 Meanwhile, preheat grill (broiler) to hot. Combine banana and honey on a baking-paper-lined oven tray. Place under grill for 5 minutes or until bananas are lightly browned and heated through.

4 Serve pancakes topped with banana and raspberries; drizzle with pan juices and extra honey, if you like.

TIPS

Sweet white sorghum flour can be found in health food stores or online. Blueberries or mixed berries would also work well instead of the raspberries. Pancakes are best served warm.

Dairy free
NUT FREE
GLUTEN FREE

**NUTRITIONAL
COUNT PER SERVING**
13.7g total fat
6.4g saturated fat
2171kJ (519 cal)
85.5g carbohydrate
13.8g protein
8.3g fibre

NUT FREE
GLUTEN FREE

NUTRITIONAL COUNT PER SERVING
31.2g total fat
6.2g saturated fat
2596kJ (621 cal)
65.9g carbohydrate
18.1g protein
9.4g fibre

Super seed bowl
WITH APPLE & YOGHURT

PREP + COOK TIME 10 MINUTES SERVES 4

- 4 medium green apples (600g), cut into matchsticks
- ⅓ cup (80ml) lemon juice
- 1 cup (250ml) coconut water
- 200g (6 ounces) strawberries, sliced thickly
- 1 cup (280g) greek-style yoghurt
- ⅓ cup (115g) honey

SUPER SEED MIX

- ⅓ cup (50g) sunflower seed kernels
- ⅓ cup (65g) pepitas (pumpkin seeds)
- ¼ cup (35g) sesame seeds
- ¼ cup (40g) poppy seeds
- ¼ cup (35g) chia seeds
- ¼ cup (35g) linseeds (flaxseeds)
- ⅓ cup (55g) currants
- ⅓ cup (40g) goji berries

1 Make super seed mix.

2 Combine apple and juice in a medium bowl.

3 Divide apple mixture and half the seed mix between four bowls, add ¼ cup (60ml) coconut water to each bowl. Top with strawberries and yoghurt; drizzle with honey and sprinkle with remaining seed mix.

super seed mix Stir sunflower seeds and pepitas in a small frying pan over medium heat for 2 minutes or until lightly golden. Add sesame seeds, poppy seeds, chia seeds and linseeds; stir for 30 seconds or until all are toasted. Remove from pan; cool. Stir in currants and goji berries. (Makes 2⅓ cups)

TIPS

Use pears instead of apples, if you like. Super seed mix can be made ahead. Store seed mix in an airtight container or jar in the fridge for up to 3 months.

Baked turkish eggs
WITH LAMB MINCE

PREP + COOK TIME 25 MINUTES **SERVES** 2

- ¼ cup (60ml) extra virgin olive oil
- 1 medium onion (150g), chopped finely
- 2 cloves garlic, crushed
- ½ teaspoon ground mixed spice
- ½ teaspoon ground cinnamon
- ¼ teaspoon chilli flakes
- 150g (4½ ounces) minced (ground) lamb
- 1 large tomato (220g), chopped coarsely
- 2 tablespoons lemon juice
- ½ teaspoon caster (superfine) sugar
- 1 tablespoon finely chopped fresh mint
- 1 tablespoon finely chopped fresh flat-leaf parsley
- 4 eggs
- ¼ cup loosely packed fresh micro mint leaves
- ¼ cup loosely packed fresh flat-leaf parsley leaves, extra
- 2 gluten-free flatbreads, quartered

CUCUMBER YOGHURT
- ½ lebanese cucumber (130g)
- ½ cup (95g) greek-style yoghurt
- 1 clove garlic, crushed
- 1 teaspoon finely grated lemon rind

1 Make cucumber yoghurt.

2 Heat 2 tablespoons of the oil in a large frying pan over medium heat; cook onion, garlic, spices and chilli flakes, for 3 minutes or until soft. Add mince; cook, breaking mince up with a wooden spoon, for 5 minutes or until browned. Add tomato, juice and sugar; cook, for 2 minutes. Remove from heat; stir in chopped herbs. Season to taste.

3 Make four indents in mince mixture with the back of a spoon. Carefully crack eggs into indents; season eggs. Cook, covered, over medium heat for a further 6 minutes or until whites of eggs have set but yolks are still runny.

4 Drizzle with remaining oil; top with cucumber yoghurt, micro mint and extra parsley. Serve with flatbread.

cucumber yoghurt Coarsely grate cucumber; squeeze out excess water. Combine cucumber with remaining ingredients in a small bowl; season to taste.

TIPS

This is a great dish for a group, just multiply the recipe. You can use minced beef, pork or chicken instead of the lamb, if you like.

NUT FREE
GLUTEN FREE

**NUTRITIONAL
COUNT PER SERVING**
51.9g total fat
14g saturated fat
4197kJ (1004 cal)
79.6g carbohydrate
49.4g protein
4.6g fibre

NUT FREE
GLUTEN FREE

**NUTRITIONAL
COUNT PER FRITTATA**
12g total fat
6.4g saturated fat
586kJ (140 cal)
0.9g carbohydrate
6.6g protein
0.7g fibre

Green power
MINI FRITTATAS

PREP + COOK TIME 35 MINUTES MAKES 8

- 2 teaspoons olive oil
- 1 small leek (200g), sliced thinly
- ½ clove garlic, crushed
- 3 cups (120g) firmly packed baby spinach leaves, chopped finely
- 5 eggs
- ½ cup (125ml) pouring cream
- 1 tablespoon finely chopped fresh mint
- 1 tablespoon finely chopped fresh basil
- 1 tablespoon finely chopped fresh dill
- 100g (3 ounces) goat's fetta, crumbled

1 Preheat oven to 180°C/350°F. Line 8 holes of a 12-hole (⅓ cup/80ml) muffin pan with paper cases.

2 Heat oil in a medium saucepan over medium heat; cook leek, stirring, for 3 minutes. Add garlic; cook for 2 minutes or until leek is soft. Add spinach; cook, stirring, 30 seconds or until wilted. Remove from heat.

3 Whisk eggs, cream and herbs in a medium jug; season.

4 Divide spinach mixture into pan holes; pour in egg mixture, then top with fetta.

5 Bake frittatas for 20 minutes or until set. Leave in pan for 5 minutes before serving warm or at room temperature.

TIPS

Store frittatas in an airtight container in the fridge for up to 5 days or freeze for up to 1 month.

Dairy free
NUT FREE
GLUTEN FREE

**NUTRITIONAL
COUNT PER SERVING**
26.5g total fat
4.9g saturated fat
1597kJ (382 cal)
23.6g carbohydrate
9g protein
6.2g fibre

**NUTRITIONAL
COUNT PER
CRACKER ONLY**
1.8g total fat
0.2g saturated fat
192kJ (46 cal)
5.7g carbohydrate
1.5g protein
0.7g fibre

Seed crackers with
SMASHED AVOCADO

PREP + COOK TIME 1½ HOURS **SERVES** 4 (MAKES 50 CRACKERS)

- 1 cup (200g) long-grain brown rice
- 2½ cups (625ml) water
- 1 cup (200g) tri-colour quinoa
- 2 cups (500ml) water, extra
- ¼ cup (40g) sesame seeds
- ¼ cup (50g) linseeds (flaxseeds)
- ¼ cup (35g) chia seeds
- ¼ cup (35g) sunflower seed kernels
- 1 tablespoon finely chopped fresh lemon thyme
- 1 tablespoon finely chopped fresh oregano
- 1 tablespoon finely chopped fresh rosemary
- 1 teaspoon cracked black pepper
- 2 teaspoons onion powder
- 2 medium avocados (500g)
- 2 tablespoons lemon juice
- 1 tablespoon chia seeds, extra
- 90g (3 ounces) snow pea shoots
- pinch sumac, optional

1 Preheat oven 180°C/350°F.

2 Place brown rice and the water in a small saucepan; bring to the boil. Reduce heat to low; simmer, uncovered, for 25 minutes or until most of the water has evaporated. Remove from heat; stand, covered, for 10 minutes. Fluff with a fork, spread out over an oven tray; cool.

3 Place quinoa and the extra water in same pan; bring to the boil. Reduce heat to low; simmer, uncovered, for 10 minutes or until most of the water has evaporated. Remove from heat; stand, covered, for 10 minutes. Fluff with a fork, spread out over an oven tray; cool.

4 Process the rice with half the quinoa to a coarse paste; transfer to a large bowl. Add remaining quinoa, the seeds, the herbs, pepper and onion powder, season; using your hands, combine well. Divide into four portions.

5 Line four oven trays with baking paper. Remove one of the pieces of baking paper. Flatten a portion of dough over paper, cover with plastic wrap then roll out with a rolling pin to 1mm-thick or as thin as possible. (Don't worry if there are holes, these will give the crackers texture and character.) Discard plastic; carefully lift the paper back onto the tray. Repeat with remaining portions of dough until you have four trays. Score the crackers into 5cm x 10cm (2-inch x 4-inch) lengths or triangles (or leave as whole sheets and break into pieces after baking).

6 Bake crackers for 20 minutes. Cover crackers with a sheet of baking paper and a second tray. Holding the hot tray with oven gloves, flip the crackers over onto the second tray; carefully remove lining paper. Repeat with remaining trays. Cook crackers for a further 20 minutes or until golden and crisp. Cool on trays.

7 To serve, roughly smash avocado with a fork in a small bowl with juice; season to taste. Place 4 crackers on each of four serving plates; top crackers with avocado mixture, extra chia seeds, snow pea shoots and sumac.

TIPS

If the cracker mixture spreads past the paper when you're rolling it just cut those edges off. If you don't have enough oven trays, you can cook the crackers in two batches. Crackers can be stored in an airtight container for up to 1 month.

Banana pancakes with
LABNE & BLUEBERRY COMPOTE

PREP + COOK TIME 40 MINUTES (+ STANDING) **SERVES 4**

You will need to start the labne 2 days ahead. If not, simply serve pancakes with the greek-style yoghurt as it is.

- 1 medium ripe banana (200g)
- ¼ cup (35g) coconut flour
- ¼ teaspoon bicarbonate of soda (baking soda)
- ¼ teaspoon ground cinnamon
- 2 eggs
- 1 vanilla bean, split lengthways, seeds scraped
- ½ cup (125ml) unsweetened almond milk
- 2 tablespoons coconut oil
- 1 medium banana (200g), extra, sliced thickly
- 2 tablespoons roasted coconut chips

LABNE

- 500g (1 pound) greek-style yoghurt
- ½ teaspoon sea salt
- 1 teaspoon finely grated lemon rind

BLUEBERRY COMPOTE

- 1 cup (250ml) apple juice
- ½ cup (75g) coconut sugar
- 2 cups (280g) frozen blueberries

1 Make labne.

2 Make blueberry compote.

3 Mash banana to a paste in a medium bowl with a fork. Add coconut flour, soda, cinnamon, eggs, vanilla seeds and almond milk; stir to combine.

4 Melt one-third of the coconut oil in a large non-stick frying pan over low-medium heat. Spoon tablespoons of batter into pan, flatten slightly; cook for 2 minutes or until bubbles appear on the surface. Using two spatulas, as mixture is delicate, carefully turn over; cook for a further 1 minute or until cooked through. Remove from pan; cover to keep warm. Repeat with remaining coconut oil and batter to make 12 pancakes in total.

5 Serve pancakes topped with labne, blueberry compote, extra banana and coconut chips.

labne Line a sieve with two layers of muslin (or a clean Chux cloth); place it over a bowl. Stir ingredients together in a small bowl; spoon into the lined sieve. Tie the cloth close to the surface of the yoghurt; refrigerate for 48 hours. (Makes 260g/8½ ounces)

blueberry compote Stir juice and coconut sugar in a medium saucepan over low heat until sugar dissolves. Bring to a simmer; cook for 10 minutes or until reduced to a thin syrup. Add frozen blueberries; stir gently until berries are coated and thawed.

GLUTEN FREE

**NUTRITIONAL
COUNT PER SERVING**
24.3g total fat
15.8g saturated fat
2337kJ (559 cal)
69.2g carbohydrate
14.3g protein
3.5g fibre

Dairy free
NUT FREE
GLUTEN FREE

**NUTRITIONAL
COUNT PER SERVING**
24.3g total fat
4.4g saturated fat
1596kJ (381 cal)
4.7g carbohydrate
30.7g protein
11.6g fibre

Mixed mushrooms with
SMOKED SALMON & EGG

PREP + COOK TIME 20 MINUTES SERVES 4

- 20g (¾ ounce) sunflower seed kernels
- 20g (¾ ounce) pepitas (pumpkin seeds)
- 2½ tablespoons olive oil
- 600g (1¼ pounds) swiss brown mushrooms, sliced thickly
- 600g (1¼ pounds) oyster mushrooms
- 1 large clove garlic, crushed
- 1 fresh long red chilli, seeded, chopped finely
- 1 tablespoon water
- 2 teaspoons lemon juice
- 1 tablespoon vinegar
- 4 free-range eggs
- 200g (6½ ounces) smoked salmon
- 2 tablespoons fresh chervil leaves

1 Heat a large frying pan over medium heat. Add sunflower seeds and pepitas; cook, stirring, for 2 minutes or until seeds are toasted. Remove from pan.

2 Heat 1 tablespoon of the oil in same pan over high heat, add half the mushrooms; cook, stirring occasionally, for 4 minutes or until browned lightly. Transfer to a large bowl; cover with foil to keep warm. Repeat with remaining oil and remaining mushrooms.

3 Return all mushrooms to pan with garlic, chilli and water; cook, stirring, for 1 minute or until fragrant. Remove from heat; stir in juice, season to taste. Transfer to a bowl; cover to keep warm.

4 Meanwhile, to poach eggs, half-fill a large, deep frying pan with water, add vinegar; bring to a gentle simmer. Break 1 egg into a cup. Using a wooden spoon, make a whirlpool in the water; slide egg into whirlpool. Repeat with remaining eggs. Cook eggs for 3 minutes or until whites are set and the yolks remain runny. Remove eggs with a slotted spoon; drain on a paper-towel-lined plate.

5 Divide mushroom mixture among plates; top with smoked salmon, eggs, seed mixture and chervil. Season.

Quinoa & pear bircher
WITH COCONUT FRUIT SALAD

PREP + COOK TIME 10 MINUTES SERVES 4

You can use grated apple or nashi instead of the pear.

- 2 tablespoons pepitas (pumpkin seeds)
- 2 tablespoons sunflower seed kernels
- 2 medium pears (460g), grated coarsely
- 3 cups (240g) quinoa flakes
- 1 cup (250ml) coconut milk
- 1 cup (250ml) unsweetened apple juice (see tips)

COCONUT FRUIT SALAD

- 2 medium young drinking coconut (1.8kg) (see tips)
- 100g (3 ounces) raspberries
- 125g (4 ounces) blueberries
- 2 tablespoons long thin strips of orange rind
- 2 medium oranges (480g), peeled, segmented (see tips)

1 Make coconut fruit salad.

2 Stir pepitas and sunflower seeds in a small frying pan over medium heat for 2 minutes or until toasted.

3 Combine pear, quinoa, coconut milk, apple juice and reserved coconut water (from coconut fruit salad) in a medium bowl.

4 Divide bircher between four serving bowls; spoon fruit salad on top. Sprinkle with toasted seeds.

coconut fruit salad Insert the tip of a small knife into the soft spot on the base of the coconut, using a twisting action. Place coconut over a glass; drain coconut water. Reserve 1 cup (250ml) for bircher. Wrap coconut in a clean towel, break open with a hammer, or by smashing it onto the floor. Spoon out the soft coconut flesh; slice into thin strips. Combine coconut flesh with remaining ingredients in a small bowl. Cover; refrigerate until required.

TIPS

Young drinking coconuts are available from green grocers and some supermarkets. To segment an orange, cut off the rind with the white pith, following the curve of the fruit. Cut down either side of each segment close to the membrane to release the segment. Look for a freshly squeezed apple juice from single variety apples such as granny smith, as they will have a clean fresh sweet and tart taste. Store bircher in an airtight container in the refrigerator for up to 4 days.

Dairy free
NUT FREE
GLUTEN FREE

**NUTRITIONAL
COUNT PER SERVING**
26.1g total fat
16.1g saturated fat
2508kJ (600 cal)
70g carbohydrate
14.5g protein
9.9g fibre

Dairy free
GLUTEN FREE

**NUTRITIONAL
COUNT PER SERVING**
88.8g total fat
49g saturated fat
3916kJ (935 cal)
21.5g carbohydrate
12.6g protein
5.6g fibre

Grain-free coconut
& VANILLA MUESLI

PREP + COOK TIME 30 MINUTES (+ COOLING) **SERVES** 4 (MAKES 4¾ CUPS)

- 2 vanilla beans
- 2½ cups (125g) flaked coconut
- ½ cup (80g) natural almonds, chopped coarsely
- ½ cup (80g) brazil nuts, chopped coarsely
- ½ cup (60g) pecans, chopped coarsely
- ¼ cup (35g) sunflower seed kernels
- ½ cup (100g) virgin coconut oil, melted
- 2 tablespoons honey
- ½ teaspoon sea salt

1 Preheat oven to 160°C/325°F. Grease and line two large oven trays with baking paper.

2 Split vanilla beans in half lengthways; using the tip of a small knife, scrape out seeds. Place seeds and pods in a large bowl with remaining ingredients; stir to combine. Spread mixture evenly between trays.

3 Bake muesli for 20 minutes, stirring occasionally to break into clumps, or until lightly golden. Cool.

TIPS

Store muesli in an airtight container in the fridge for up to 4 weeks. Serve with milk or yoghurt. To keep this dairy-free serve with your favourite milk alternative.

Breakfast salad with
POACHED EGGS & KALE PESTO

PREP + COOK TIME 25 MINUTES **SERVES** 4

- 1½ cups (45g) firmly packed baby leaves (see tips)
- 200g (6 ounces) brussels sprouts, shaved thinly
- 2 cups (300g) crunchy combo sprout mix
- 1 medium carrot (120g), cut into matchsticks
- ¼ cup (35g) toasted sunflower seed kernels
- ¼ cup (60ml) apple cider vinegar
- 2½ tablespoons avocado oil
- 2 teaspoons honey
- 1½ tablespoons white vinegar
- 8 eggs
- 1 medium avocado (250g), sliced thinly

KALE PESTO
- ⅓ cup (55g) dry-roasted almonds
- ⅓ cup (50g) roasted cashews
- 2 small cloves garlic
- 2 cups (80g) baby kale, chopped coarsely
- ½ cup (125ml) extra virgin olive oil
- 1½ tablespoons apple cider vinegar
- ¼ cup (20g) finely grated parmesan

1 Make kale pesto.

2 Place baby leaves, brussels sprouts, sprout mix, carrot and seeds in a medium bowl; toss to combine. Whisk cider vinegar, 1 tablespoon of the oil and honey in a small bowl; season to taste. Add dressing to salad; toss to combine.

3 To poach eggs, half-fill a large, deep-frying pan with water, add white vinegar; bring to a gentle simmer. Break 1 egg into a cup. Using a wooden spoon, make a whirlpool in the water; slide egg into whirlpool. Repeat with 3 more eggs. Cook eggs for 3 minutes or until whites are set and the yolks are runny. Remove eggs with a slotted spoon; drain on a paper-towel-lined plate. Repeat poaching with remaining eggs.

4 Divide salad between serving bowls; top with avocado and eggs. Spoon pesto on eggs; drizzle with remaining oil.

kale pesto Pulse nuts and garlic in a food processor until coarsely chopped. Add kale, oil and vinegar; pulse to a fine paste. Add parmesan, season; pulse until just combined. (Makes 1¼ cups)

TIPS

We used a baby leaf micro herb mix of sorrel, parsley, coriander (cilantro) and radish. Leftover pesto can be stored, covered with a thin layer of oil, in an airtight container in the fridge for up to 1 week.

GLUTEN FREE

NUTRITIONAL COUNT PER SERVING
77.6g total fat
14.1g saturated fat
3560kJ (850 cal)
9.8g carbohydrate
25.3g protein
8.9g fibre

NUT FREE
GLUTEN FREE

**NUTRITIONAL
COUNT PER SERVING**
56g total fat
11g saturated fat
2969kJ (709 cal)
27g carbohydrate
22.5g protein
6.6g fibre

Vegie & egg POWER STACK

PREP + COOK TIME 40 MINUTES SERVES 4

- 400g (12½ ounces) medium kumara (orange sweet potato) (see tips)
- 8 fresh shiitake mushrooms (140g), stems trimmed
- ¼ cup (60ml) olive oil
- 2 teaspoons chopped fresh rosemary
- 1 long fresh red chilli, seeded, chopped
- 2 tablespoons sunflower seed kernels
- 2 cups (80g) baby kale
- ¼ cup (20g) finely grated parmesan
- 1 tablespoon white vinegar
- 8 fresh eggs
- 3 green heirloom tomatoes (380g), sliced (see tips)
- 4 baby target beetroot (beets) (80g), sliced thinly (see tips)
- ½ cup baby micro cress

LEMON AÏOLI

- 1 egg yolk
- 1 small clove garlic, chopped
- 1 tablespoon finely grated lemon rind
- 1 teaspoon fresh chopped rosemary
- 2 tablespoons lemon juice
- ½ teaspoon honey
- ½ cup (125ml) olive oil

1 Preheat oven to 200°C/400°F. Line an oven tray with baking paper.

2 Cut kumara into eight 5mm (¼-inch) thick rounds. Place on tray with mushrooms, 2 tablespoons of the oil, rosemary and chilli; toss to coat. Bake for 25 minutes or until kumara is tender.

3 Meanwhile, make lemon aïoli.

4 Heat remaining oil in a medium frying pan over medium heat; cook sunflower seeds, stirring, for 2 minutes or until toasted. Stir in kale, turn off heat; leave for the residual heat to wilt leaves. Add parmesan; season to taste.

5 To poach eggs, half-fill a large, deep-frying pan with water, add vinegar; bring to a gentle simmer. Break 1 egg into a cup. Using a wooden spoon, make a whirlpool in the water; slide egg into whirlpool. Repeat with 3 more eggs. Cook eggs for 3 minutes or until whites are set and the yolks are runny. Remove eggs with a slotted spoon; drain on a paper-towel-lined plate. Repeat poaching with remaining eggs.

6 Spoon 2 tablespoons of the aïoli onto each plate. Build two stacks on each plate with kumara, tomato, mushrooms then kale mixture. Top each stack with a poached egg, sliced beetroot and micro cress.

lemon aïoli Process egg yolk, garlic, rind, rosemary, juice and honey in a small food processor for 1 minute. With motor operating, gradually add oil, drop by drop at first, then in a slow steady stream until mixture is thick and emulsified. Season to taste. (Makes ⅔ cup)

TIPS

Try to buy a kumara with a diameter of 7cm (2¾ inches) as it will provide the base for your stack, and tomatoes of a similar size. If heirloom green tomatoes are hard to find, use red. Target beetroots are available from specialist green grocers and grower's markets. If they're unavailable, use radishes or a little shaved fennel instead.

Baked ricotta with caramelised
ONIONS & FLATBREAD

PREP + COOK TIME 50 MINUTES **SERVES** 2

- 250g (8 ounces) ricotta
- 1 egg, beaten lightly
- 1 tablespoon chopped fresh oregano
- 2 teaspoons olive oil
- 1 small brown onion (80g), sliced thinly
- 1 teaspoon butter
- ½ teaspoon brown sugar
- 2 teaspoons balsamic vinegar
- 2 gluten-free flatbread (see tips) or pizza bases

1 Preheat oven to 200°C/400°F. Grease a 6cm x 12.5cm (2½-inch x 5-inch) (base measurement) loaf pan; line base and long sides with baking paper, extending the paper 5cm (2 inches) over the sides.

2 Combine ricotta, egg and oregano in a medium bowl; season. Spoon mixture into pan, smooth surface; place on an oven tray. Bake for 25 minutes or until ricotta mixture has risen and is set.

3 Meanwhile, heat oil in a medium frying pan over low heat; cook onion, stirring occasionally, for 10 minutes or until onion softens and is browned lightly. Increase heat to high, add butter, sugar and vinegar; cook, stirring, for 3 minutes or until sugar dissolves and mixture thickens slightly. Season.

4 Place flatbread on a heated oiled grill pan (or grill or barbecue) for 1 minute each side or until browned.

5 Spoon onion mixture onto baked ricotta; serve with heated flatbread.

TIPS

Baked ricotta can be made a day ahead; cover, refrigerate. You can use basil or parsley instead of oregano, if you like. To make your own flatbread, follow the recipe on page 82.

**NUTRITIONAL
COUNT PER SERVING**
25.3g total fat
10.3g saturated fat
2819kJ (673 cal)
90.7g carbohydrate
18.4g protein
1g fibre

GLUTEN FREE

**NUTRITIONAL
COUNT PER SERVING**
24.3g total fat
5.9g saturated fat
1438kJ (344 cal)
12.5g carbohydrate
18g protein
1.8g fibre

Strawberry & almond
SWEET FRITTATA

PREP + COOK TIME 30 MINUTES **SERVES** 4

- 250g (8 ounces) strawberries, hulled
- 1 tablespoon coconut sugar
- 1 vanilla bean
- 6 eggs
- 2 tablespoons coconut sugar, extra
- ⅓ cup (40g) ground almonds
- 10g (½ ounce) butter
- 100g (3 ounces) firm ricotta, crumbled coarsely
- ⅓ cup (55g) dry-roasted almonds, chopped coarsely

1 Thinly slice half the strawberries; cut remaining strawberries in half. Combine halved strawberries with coconut sugar in a small bowl. Reserve sliced strawberries.

2 Split vanilla bean lengthways; using the tip of a knife, scrape the seeds. Reserve pod for another use (see tips).

3 Place vanilla seeds, eggs, extra coconut sugar and ground almonds in a medium bowl; whisk until combined.

4 Preheat grill (broiler) to high.

5 Melt butter in a 24cm (9½-inch) non-stick ovenproof frying pan over medium heat. Add egg mixture, top with sliced strawberries, ricotta and half the chopped almonds. Reduce heat to low; cook for 8 minutes or until half set. Place pan under grill for a further 8 minutes or until ricotta is lightly browned and mixture is just set.

6 Serve frittata immediately topped with halved strawberries and remaining chopped almonds. If you like, drizzle with a little honey and sprinkle with black chia seeds.

TIPS

The unused vanilla pod can be wrapped and frozen for up to 1 year. Use in recipes where a vanilla bean is called for. You can use macadamias and hazelnuts instead of the almonds, if you like.

Coconut porridge with
MAPLE BAKED PEARS

PREP + COOK TIME 20 MINUTES SERVES 4

- 2 medium beurre bosc pears (460g), halved
- 2 tablespoons pure maple syrup
- ¼ cup (40g) almond kernels, chopped coarsely
- 2 cups (220g) quinoa flakes
- 1 litre (4 cups) coconut milk
- 1 tablespoon brown sugar
- 2 tablespoons pure maple syrup, extra
- ⅓ cup (10g) flaked coconut, toasted

1 Preheat oven to 180°C/350°F.

2 Place pears on a baking-paper-lined oven tray; drizzle with maple syrup. Bake for 25 minutes or until pears are golden and tender. Add almonds for the last 5 minutes of pear cooking time.

3 Meanwhile, place quinoa, coconut milk and sugar in a medium saucepan over medium heat; cook, stirring, for 6 minutes or until cooked and creamy.

4 Serve porridge topped with baked pears, almonds and any pan juices; drizzle with extra maple syrup and top with flaked coconut.

TIPS

Quinoa flakes must be fully cooked before eating; make sure they are tender.

Dairy free
GLUTEN FREE

**NUTRITIONAL
COUNT PER SERVING**
15.5g total fat
7.2g saturated fat
2038kJ (487 cal)
76g carbohydrate
9g protein
1.4g fibre

4 ways with LOAVES

Dairy free
NUT FREE
GLUTEN FREE

NUTRITIONAL COUNT PER SERVING
16.3g total fat
8.4g saturated fat
1827kJ (437 cal)
67.8g carbohydrate
4.7g protein
2.9g fibre

NUTRITIONAL COUNT PER SERVING
12.1g total fat
9.6g saturated fat
1443kJ (345 cal)
54.9g carbohydrate
3.9g protein
2.1g fibre

Dairy free
NUT FREE
GLUTEN FREE

BEETROOT & CACAO LOAF

PREP + COOK TIME 1½ HOURS
(+ COOLING) SERVES 8

You will need 450g (14½oz) canned baby beetroot for this recipe.

Preheat oven to 180°C/350°F. Grease a 12cm x 22cm (4¾-in x 9-in) loaf pan (base measure); line base and long sides with baking paper extending the paper 5cm (2in) over the sides. Place ¾ cup (100g) gluten-free plain (all-purpose) flour, 1 cup (135g) gluten-free self-raising flour, ½ cup (75g) buckwheat flour, 1½ teaspoons gluten-free baking powder, ¼ cup (55g) caster (superfine) sugar and ¼ cup (25g) sifted cacao powder in a large bowl with 3 lightly beaten eggs, 1¼ cups (320g) mashed overripe banana, 1 cup (230g) blended drained canned beetroot, ½ cup (125ml) maple syrup, 1 teaspoon vanilla essence and ¼ cup (60ml) light olive oil; stir until combined. Pour into pan, smooth surface. Bake loaf for 1 hour 20 minutes or until a skewer inserted comes out clean. Stand in pan for 5 minutes; turn onto a wire rack to cool. Stir ¼ cup (60ml) melted coconut oil, ¼ cup (35g) cacao powder and 2 tablespoons maple syrup in a bowl until smooth; stand until thickened and spreadable. Spread on cooled loaf.

TIP Cooled loaf can be sliced and individual slices wrapped in plastic wrap and frozen for up to 3 months.

MANGO & COCONUT LOAF

PREP + COOK TIME 1¾ HOURS
(+ COOLING) SERVES 8

Frozen chopped mango pieces are available from supermarkets.

Preheat oven to 180°C/350°F. Grease a 12cm x 22cm (4¾-in x 9-in) loaf pan (base measure); line base and long sides with baking paper extending the paper 5cm (2in) over the sides. Place ½ cup (65g) gluten-free plain (all-purpose) flour, 1 cup (135g) gluten-free self-raising flour, ½ cup (75g) buckwheat flour, 1½ teaspoons gluten-free baking powder, ¼ cup (55g) caster (superfine) sugar and ½ cup (40g) desiccated coconut in a large bowl with 3 lightly beaten eggs, ⅓ cup (80ml) maple syrup, 1¼ cups (320g) mashed overripe banana, 1 cup (200g) coarsely chopped frozen mango, 1 teaspoon vanilla essence and ¼ cup (60ml) melted coconut oil; stir until combined. Pour into pan, smooth surface. Bake loaf for 1½ hours or until a skewer inserted comes out clean. Stand in pan for 5 minutes; turn onto a wire rack to cool.

TIP Cooled loaf can be sliced and individual slices wrapped in plastic wrap and frozen for up to 3 months.

NUT FREE
GLUTEN FREE

Dairy free
NUT FREE
GLUTEN FREE

**NUTRITIONAL
COUNT PER SERVING**
8.8g total fat
1.7g saturated fat
1556kJ (372 cal)
68.5g carbohydrate
4.3g protein
2.2g fibre

**NUTRITIONAL
COUNT PER SERVING**
8.9g total fat
1.7g saturated fat
1560kJ (373 cal)
68.5g carbohydrate
4.3g protein
2.6g fibre

BANANA & MAPLE SYRUP LOAF

PREP + COOK TIME 1¾ HOURS SERVES 8

You will need to mash 5 large overripe bananas for this recipe.

Preheat oven to 180°C/350°F. Grease a 12cm x 22cm (4¾-in x 9-in) loaf pan (base measure); line base and long sides with baking paper extending the paper 5cm (2in) over the sides. Place 1 cup (135g) gluten-free plain (all-purpose) flour, 1 cup (135g) gluten-free self-raising flour, ½ cup (75g) buckwheat flour, 1½ teaspoons gluten-free baking powder and ¼ cup (55g) caster (superfine) sugar in a large bowl with 3 lightly beaten eggs, 2¼ cups (580g) mashed overripe banana, ⅓ cup (80ml) maple syrup, 1 teaspoon vanilla essence and ¼ cup (60ml) light olive oil; stir until well combined. Pour into pan, smooth surface. Top with 1 large (230g) banana sliced lengthways and brush with 1 tablespoon maple syrup. Bake loaf for 1½ hours or until a skewer inserted comes out clean (cover top with foil to prevent over browning during baking). Stand in pan for 5 minutes; turn onto a wire rack to cool.

TIP Cooled loaf can be sliced and individual slices wrapped in plastic wrap and frozen for up to 3 months.

FIG & CINNAMON LOAF

**PREP + COOK TIME 1¾ HOURS
(+ COOLING) SERVES 8**

You will need to mash 5 large overripe bananas for this recipe.

Preheat oven to 180°C/350°F. Grease a 12cm x 22cm (4¾-in x 9-in) loaf pan (base measure); line base and long sides with baking paper extending the paper 5cm (2in) over the sides. Place 1 cup (135g) gluten-free plain (all-purpose) flour, 1 cup (135g) gluten-free self-raising flour, ½ cup (75g) buckwheat flour, 1½ teaspoons gluten-free baking powder, ¼ cup (55g) caster (superfine) sugar and 1½ teaspoons ground cinnamon in a large bowl with 3 lightly beaten eggs, 2¼ cups (580g) mashed overripe banana, 1 cup (140g) chopped fresh figs, ⅓ cup (80ml) maple syrup, 1 teaspoon vanilla essence and ¼ cup (60ml) light olive oil; stir until well combined. Pour into pan, smooth surface. Bake loaf for 1½ hours or until a skewer inserted comes out clean. Brush top of loaf with 1 tablespoon maple syrup during baking. Stand in pan for 5 minutes; turn onto a wire rack to cool.

TIP Cooled loaf can be sliced and individual slices wrapped in plastic wrap and frozen for up to 3 months.

Lunch

Chunky fried
CAULIFLOWER RICE

PREP + COOK TIME 35 MINUTES **SERVES** 4

- 500g (1 pound) cauliflower, cut into florets
- 2 teaspoons coconut oil, plus 1 tablespoon extra
- 2 eggs, beaten lightly
- 2 cloves garlic, crushed
- 1 teaspoon finely grated fresh ginger
- 2 fresh small red thai (serrano) chillies, seeded, sliced thinly
- 1 medium red capsicum (bell pepper) (200g), sliced thinly
- 80g (2½ ounces) baby sweet corn, halved
- 100g (3 ounces) fresh shiitake mushrooms, sliced
- 150g (4½ ounces) sugar snap peas, halved lengthways
- 2 tablespoons gluten-free tamari
- 6 green onions (scallions), sliced thinly
- ¼ cup fresh coriander (cilantro) leaves

1 Pulse cauliflower in a food processer until chopped coarsely.

2 Heat coconut oil in a large deep frying pan or wok; pour in half the egg, swirl around the base of the pan to make a thin omelette. Cook, uncovered, for 2 minutes or until egg is just set. Remove from pan; roll tightly, cut into thin strips. Repeat with remaining egg.

3 Heat extra oil in same pan over medium heat; cook garlic, ginger and chilli, stirring for 2 minutes or until fragrant. Add cauliflower; cook, stirring, over high heat for 5 minutes or until cauliflower starts to colour.

4 Add capsicum and corn; cook, stirring for 2 minutes or until capsicum starts to soften. Add mushrooms and peas; cook, stirring for a further 2 minutes. Stir in tamari and green onion; cook, stirring, until combined and heated through. Season. Remove from pan.

5 Serve cauliflower rice topped with omelette strips and coriander leaves.

TIPS

Omit cauliflower and serve with ¾ cup (150g) brown rice boiled for 25 minutes or until tender.

Dairy free
NUT FREE
GLUTEN FREE

**NUTRITIONAL
COUNT PER SERVING**
9.7g total fat
7.1g saturated fat
750kJ (179 cal)
9.3g carbohydrate
9.8g protein
7.4g fibre

Nut free
EGG FREE
GLUTEN FREE

NUTRITIONAL
COUNT PER SLIDER
13g total fat
3.2g saturated fat
903kJ (216 cal)
15.1g carbohydrate
8.4g protein
3g fibre

Prawn & crab
SWEET POTATO SLIDERS

PREP + COOK TIME 35 MINUTES **MAKES** 12

The sweet potatoes need to be about 7cm (2¾ inches) in diameter, as they will serve as the 'buns' for the sliders.

- 3 purple-skinned white-fleshed sweet potatoes (1kg), unpeeled
- ¼ cup (60ml) olive oil
- 12 large green king prawns (shrimp) (300g), peeled, deveined, with tails intact
- 2 cups (50g) watercress sprigs
- ¼ cup fresh micro sorrel leaves
- ¼ cup fresh coriander (cilantro) leaves
- 1 tablespoon extra virgin olive oil
- 1 tablespoon lemon juice
- 1 medium avocado (250g)

CRAB FILLING

- 200g (6½ ounces) cooked crab meat
- ½ cup (60g) crème fraîche
- ½ clove garlic, crushed
- 1 green onion (scallion), chopped finely
- 1 tablespoon finely chopped fresh chives
- 1 tablespoon nigella seeds
- 2 tablespoons horseradish cream
- 1 tablespoon lemon juice

1 Cut eight 8mm (½-inch) thick rounds, from each sweet potato (you need 24 rounds in total); discard tapered ends. Brush rounds with 2 tablespoons of the olive oil; season. Cook rounds, in batches, on a heated grill plate (or barbecue) for 6 minutes each side or until cooked through. Remove from heat; keep warm.

2 Make crab filling.

3 Coat prawns in remaining olive oil; season. Cook prawns on heated grill plate for 1 minute each side or until just cooked through. Remove from heat; cover to keep warm.

4 Place watercress, sorrel and coriander in a small bowl with extra virgin olive oil and juice, season; toss gently to combine. Mash avocado in a small bowl.

5 Place 12 sweet potato rounds on a board; top each with crab filling, a prawn, mashed avocado and watercress salad. Top with remaining sweet potato rounds.

crab filling Combine ingredients in a small bowl; season.

TIPS

We used crème fraîche in the crab filling rather than a commercial aïoli or mayonnaise. For a dairy-free option use your favourite dairy-free mayonnaise.

Italian white bean
& CABBAGE SOUP

PREP + COOK TIME 1¼ HOURS (+ REFRIGERATION & STANDING) **SERVES** 4

You will need to start this recipe a day ahead.

- 1½ cups (300g) dried cannellini beans
- 2 teaspoons olive oil
- 1 medium brown onion (150g), chopped coarsely
- 2 stalks celery (300g), chopped coarsely
- 2 cloves garlic, sliced thinly
- 2 litres (8 cups) gluten-free vegetable stock
- 2 slices gluten-free prosciutto (30g)
- 400g (12½ ounces) cabbage, shredded finely
- 3 teaspoons lemon juice
- ¼ cup fresh flat-leaf parsley leaves

1 Place beans in a medium bowl, cover with water; stand overnight. Rinse under cold water; drain.

2 Heat oil in a large saucepan over medium heat; cook onion, celery and garlic, stirring, for 5 minutes or until softened. Add stock and beans to the pan; bring to the boil. Reduce heat; simmer, covered, for 50 minutes or until beans are tender.

3 Cook prosciutto in a non-stick frying pan, over high heat, for 1 minute each side or until crisp; break into shards.

4 Add cabbage to soup; simmer, covered, for 5 minutes or until just wilted. Stir in juice. Serve soup topped with prosciutto and parsley leaves.

TIPS

Soak a large quantity of beans and boil until tender, store in the freezer in airtight bags so that you have beans on hand. You can use thinly sliced bacon or leftover roasted chicken instead of prosciutto. Add some finely shredded fresh sage leaves when frying the onion, if you like.

Dairy free
NUT FREE
GLUTEN FREE
EGG FREE

**NUTRITIONAL
COUNT PER SERVING**
4.7g total fat
1g saturated fat
1200kJ (287 cal)
36.5g carbohydrate
19.4g protein
15.5g fibre

Dairy free
EGG FREE
GLUTEN FREE

**NUTRITIONAL
COUNT PER SERVING**
15.3g total fat
3.5g saturated fat
1973kJ (471 cal)
41.7g carbohydrate
36.3g protein
11.1g fibre

Rocket, chicken & DATE SALAD

PREP + COOK TIME 40 MINUTES (+ COOLING) SERVES 4

- 600g (1¼ pounds) chicken breast fillet, trimmed
- 1.5 litres (6 cups) water
- 2 large oranges (600g)
- ¼ cup (60ml) lemon juice
- 1 tablespoon fresh lemon thyme leaves
- 1 tablespoon extra virgin olive oil
- 1 medium pomegranate (380g), halved crossways
- 150g (4½ ounces) baby rocket (arugula) leaves
- 8 fresh dates (160g), seeded, quartered lengthways
- 24 dry roasted natural almonds (15g), chopped coarsely

1 Place chicken and the water in a medium saucepan over high heat; bring to the boil. Reduce heat to low; simmer, uncovered, for 10 minutes. Remove pan from heat; cool chicken in poaching liquid for 20 minutes.

2 Meanwhile, using a zester, remove rind from 1 orange into long thin strips. Peel both oranges, cut into segments, reserving ¼ cup (60ml) of juice.

3 To make dressing, combine juices, rind, thyme and oil in a small jug. Season with pepper.

4 Remove seeds from pomegranate (see tips); reserve.

5 Remove chicken from poaching liquid; shred coarsely.

6 Arrange rocket on a large serving plate. Drizzle with a little dressing. Top with chicken, orange segments, dates, pomegranate seeds and almonds. Serve salad drizzled with remaining dressing.

TIPS

The chicken can be cooked a day ahead; refrigerate, covered, until required. If you don't have a zester, use a peeler to cut strips of orange rind, then cut the rind into thin strips. To remove the seeds from the pomegranate, hold each half, cut-side down, in the palm of your hand over a bowl, then hit the outside firmly with a wooden spoon. The seeds should fall out easily; discard any white pith that falls out with them.

Mushroom, garlic & FETTA FRITTATA

PREP + COOK TIME 35 MINUTES (+ STANDING) **SERVES** 4

- 1 tablespoon olive oil
- 2 x 150g (4½-ounce) packets pasta mushroom mix (see tips), chopped coarsely
- 1 clove garlic, crushed
- 10 eggs
- 100g (3 ounces) fetta, crumbled
- 260g (8½ ounces) cherry or baby roma (egg) truss tomatoes
- 40g (1½ ounces) baby kale

CARAMELISED ONIONS

- 1 tablespoon olive oil
- 2 medium brown onions (300g), sliced thinly
- 1 tablespoon brown sugar
- 1 tablespoon red wine vinegar

1 Preheat oven to 180°C/350°F. Grease a deep 19cm (8-inch) square cake pan; line base and sides with baking paper extending the paper 5cm (2 inches) over the sides.

2 Heat oil in a medium frying pan over medium heat; cook mushrooms and garlic, stirring, for 2 minutes or until mushrooms are tender. Remove from heat.

3 Whisk eggs in a large bowl until combined; season. Pour eggs into cake pan; top with mushroom mixture and fetta.

4 Place tomatoes on an oiled oven tray. Bake frittata and tomatoes for 20 minutes or until frittata is cooked through and tomatoes have softened. Leave frittata in pan for 5 minutes before serving.

5 Meanwhile, make caramelised onions.

6 Serve frittata topped with caramelised onions, roasted tomatoes and kale.

caramelised onions Heat oil in a medium frying pan over medium heat; cook onions, stirring occasionally, for 10 minutes or until golden brown. Stir in sugar and vinegar; cook for a further 3 minutes or until caramelised.

TIPS

Pasta mushroom mix contains king brown, enoki and shimeji mushrooms. You can use a combination of your favourite mushrooms. This frittata is great for a portable work or school lunch as it can be eaten cold.

NUT FREE
GLUTEN FREE

**NUTRITIONAL
COUNT PER SERVING**
28.3g total fat
9.2g saturated fat
1685kJ (403 cal)
9.6g carbohydrate
25.5g protein
4.8g fibre

Dairy free
EGG FREE
GLUTEN FREE

**NUTRITIONAL
COUNT PER SERVING**
5.8g total fat
0.8g saturated fat
781kJ (187 cal)
21.2g carbohydrate
7.8g protein
8.1g fibre

Vegetable LARB

PREP + COOK TIME 30 MINUTES (+ STANDING) **SERVES 4**

- 2 tablespoons fish sauce or gluten-free tamari
- 2 tablespoons lime juice
- ½ teaspoon dried chilli flakes
- 1 medium beetroot (beet) (160g), peeled, cut into 5mm (¼-inch) pieces
- 1 large carrot (180g), unpeeled, cut into 5mm (¼-inch) pieces
- 160g (5 ounces) snake beans (see tips), cut into 5mm (¼-inch) pieces
- 1 lebanese cucumber (130g), halved lengthways
- ¼ cup (50g) jasmine rice
- 200g (6½ ounces) small cherry tomatoes, halved
- 3 green onions (scallions), sliced thinly
- ½ cup finely chopped fresh mint
- 2 tablespoons finely chopped fresh thai basil or coriander (cilantro)
- ⅓ cup (45g) roasted unsalted peanuts, chopped finely
- 1 medium butter (boston) lettuce, leaves separated

1 Preheat oven to 180°C/350°F.

2 Combine fish sauce, juice and chilli flakes in a large bowl.

3 Combine beetroot and 1 tablespoon of the dressing in a small bowl. Combine carrot, snake beans and another 2 tablespoons of the dressing in a medium bowl. Remove seeds from cucumber; cut into 5mm (¼-inch) pieces. Add cucumber to remaining dressing in large bowl. Cover each bowl with plastic wrap; stand vegetables for 15 minutes.

4 Meanwhile, place rice on an oven tray; roast in oven for 12 minutes or until golden. Process rice in a small food processor (or crush with a mortar and pestle) until very finely crushed.

5 Add tomatoes to cucumber mixture with green onion, herbs, ground rice, carrot mixture and half the peanuts. Strain beetroot mixture through a sieve, add to larb; toss gently to combine.

6 Serve vegetable larb with lettuce leaves, topped with remaining peanuts.

TIPS

You will need about half a bunch of snake beans for this recipe. This salad is great for a portable work lunch; transport in an airtight container and keep refrigerated.

Indian spiced chickpea bites
WITH MINT & ROCKET SALAD

PREP + COOK TIME 40 MINUTES SERVES 4

- 1 tablespoon vegetable oil
- 1 medium brown onion (150g), chopped finely
- 1 clove garlic, crushed
- 4 fresh curry leaves
- 2 teaspoons ground cumin
- 2 teaspoons ground coriander
- ½ teaspoon fennel seeds
- ½ teaspoon turmeric
- 400g (12½ ounces) canned chickpeas (garbanzo beans), drained, rinsed
- ¼ cup (30g) ground almonds
- 2 eggs
- vegetable oil, extra, for shallow-frying
- 100g (3 ounces) baby rocket (arugula) leaves
- 1 small red onion (100g), sliced thinly
- ½ cup fresh mint leaves
- 1 fresh small red thai (serrano) chilli, seeded, sliced thinly
- ½ cup (140g) greek-style yoghurt
- 2 tablespoons mango chutney
- 1½ tablespoons water

1 Heat oil in a medium frying pan over medium heat; cook onion and garlic, stirring, for 5 minutes or until soft. Add curry leaves and spices; cook, stirring, for 1 minute or until fragrant. Remove from heat; cool.

2 Process onion mixture with chickpeas, almonds and egg until mixture is just combined. Shape tablespoons of mixture into patties.

3 Heat enough oil to come 2cm (¾-inch) up the sides of a medium frying pan over medium heat. Shallow-fry level tablespoons of chickpea mixture 2-3 minutes each side or until golden and cooked through. Drain on paper towel.

4 Place rocket, onion, mint and chilli in a large bowl with patties; toss gently to combine. Combine yoghurt, chutney and the water in a small bowl mix.

5 Serve salad with yoghurt mixture and, if you like, lime wedges.

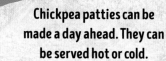

TIPS

Chickpea patties can be made a day ahead. They can be served hot or cold.

GLUTEN FREE

**NUTRITIONAL
COUNT PER SERVING**
27.6g total fat
4.6g saturated fat
1675kJ (400 cal)
22.3g carbohydrate
13.1g protein
6.6g fibre

**NUTRITIONAL
COUNT PER SERVING**
26.8g total fat
10.7g saturated fat
2484kJ (593 cal)
51.1g carbohydrate
33.9g protein
6.4g fibre

ZUCCHINI & QUINOA SLICE

PREP + COOK TIME 1 HOUR SERVES 4

- 1½ cups (300g) quinoa
- 1½ cups (375ml) water
- 2 teaspoons olive oil
- 3 rindless bacon rashers (195g), chopped coarsely
- 1 medium brown onion (150g), chopped finely
- 2 medium zucchini (240g), grated coarsely
- 5 eggs, beaten lightly
- 1 cup (100g) coarsely grated tasty cheese
- 1½ tablespoons french mustard

1 Preheat oven to 180°C/350°F. Grease a 20cm x 30cm (8-inchx 12-inch) rectangular slice pan; line base and long sides with baking paper, extending the paper 5cm (2 inches) over the sides.

2 Rinse quinoa under cold running water until water runs clear; drain well. Place quinoa in a medium saucepan with the water over high heat; bring to the boil. Reduce heat to low; cook, covered, for 15 minutes or until liquid is absorbed. Cool.

3 Meanwhile, heat oil in a medium non-stick frying pan; cook bacon and onion over medium heat, stirring, for 5 minutes or until onion is soft.

4 Place quinoa and bacon mixture in a large bowl, add remaining ingredients; stir until combined. Pour mixture into pan; smooth the surface.

5 Bake slice for 40 minutes or until browned and firm to touch. Cool in pan. Cut slice into 8 squares. Serve topped with micro herbs, if you like.

serving suggestion Serve with chilli sauce and a mixed leaf salad.

TIPS

This slice can be cooked the day before and packed into lunch boxes for school or work. Store covered in the fridge.

Ginger & chilli chicken
RICE PAPER ROLLS

PREP TIME 20 MINUTES **SERVES** 4

- 100g (3 ounces) rice vermicelli noodles
- 2 tablespoons finely grated ginger
- 2 teaspoons rice bran oil
- 1 tablespoon lime juice
- 1 tablespoon chinese cooking wine (shao hsing)
- 4 skinless cooked chicken breast fillets (800g), sliced thickly
- 12 x 22cm (9-inch) rice paper rounds
- 24 fresh coriander (cilantro) sprigs
- 1 medium carrot (120g), grated coarsely
- 4 green onions (scallions), halved lengthways, cut into matchsticks
- 1 small red capsicum (bell pepper) (300g), cut into matchsticks
- 1 lebanese cucumber (130g), cut into matchsticks
- 1 long red chilli, seeded, sliced thinly
- ⅔ cup (50g) bean sprouts

1 Place noodles in a large heatproof bowl; cover with boiling water, separate noodles with a fork. Stand until tender; drain.

2 Place ginger in a fine sieve over a medium bowl, press down firmly on ginger to remove juice; discard pulp. Add oil, lime juice and cooking wine to ginger juice, then add chicken and noodles; toss gently until combined.

3 Working with one rice paper round at a time, dip round into a bowl of warm water until soft. Lift sheet from water; place on a clean tea towel. Place two coriander sprigs on the rice paper, top with one-twelfth of the noodle mixture, carrot, green onion, capsicum, cucumber, chilli and sprouts. Fold rice sheet over filling, then fold in both sides. Continue rolling to enclose filling. Repeat with remaining rice paper rounds and filling ingredients to make a total of 12 rolls. Serve with lime wedges, if you like.

TIPS

Rice paper rolls can be prepared up to 1 day ahead of serving. Cover with damp paper towel and plastic wrap; keep refrigerated. You can use poached chicken breast or the breast from a barbecued or roasted chicken.

Dairy free
NUT FREE
GLUTEN FREE
EGG FREE

**NUTRITIONAL
COUNT PER SERVING**
14g total fat
3.8g saturated fat
1976kJ (472 cal)
36.1g carbohydrate
46.3g protein
4g fibre

GLUTEN
FREE

**NUTRITIONAL
COUNT PER SERVING**
28.5g total fat
6g saturated fat
1606kJ (384 cal)
17.7g carbohydrate
10g protein
8g fibre

Zucchini & ricotta fritters
WITH CARROT RELISH

PREP + COOK TIME 40 MINUTES **SERVES** 4

- 600g (1¼ pounds) zucchini, grated coarsely
- 1 tablespoon sea salt flakes
- 2 cloves garlic, crushed
- 2 green onions (scallions), chopped finely
- 2 tablespoons coarsely chopped fresh mint
- 2 eggs
- 2 teaspoons finely grated lemon rind
- ¾ cup (90g) ground almonds
- ½ cup (120g) firm ricotta
- ¼ cup (60ml) olive oil
- 100g (3 ounces) baby rocket (arugula)

CARROT RELISH

- 2 tablespoons olive oil
- 2 cloves garlic, crushed
- ¼ teaspoon chilli flakes
- 3 medium carrots (360g), cut into thin matchsticks
- ¼ cup (40g) currants
- 2 tablespoons norbu (monk fruit sugar)
- ¼ cup (60ml) red wine vinegar
- ½ cup (125ml) water
- 1 teaspoon ground cardamom
- 400g (12½ ounces) vine-ripened tomatoes, seeded, chopped coarsely

1 Combine zucchini and salt in a medium bowl. Stand for 15 minutes.

2 Meanwhile, make carrot relish.

3 Squeeze excess liquid from zucchini. Combine zucchini with garlic, green onion, mint, eggs, rind, ground almonds and ricotta in a medium bowl; season.

4 Heat half the oil in a large frying pan over medium heat. Pour heaped ¼-cups of fritter mixture into pan; cook for 3 minutes each side or until golden and cooked through. Remove from pan; cover to keep warm. Repeat with remaining oil and fritter mixture to make 12 fritters in total.

5 Serve fritters topped with relish and rocket.

carrot relish Heat oil in a large frying pan over medium-high heat; cook garlic and chilli flakes for 30 seconds. Add carrot; cook for 3 minutes. Stir in currants, norbu, vinegar, the water and cardamom; cook for 6 minutes or until liquid has evaporated. Stir in tomatoes; cook a further 2 minutes or until softened slightly. Season. Cool.

Spiced vegetable, chickpea
& RICOTTA SALAD

PREP + COOK TIME 1 HOUR **SERVES** 4

- 400g (12½ ounces) baby carrots, trimmed
- 1 medium kumara (orange sweet potato) (400g), cut into 2cm (¾-inch) wedges
- 1 small red onion (100g), cut into wedges
- 1 medium red capsicum (bell pepper) (350g), sliced thickly
- 400g (12½ ounces) canned chickpeas (garbanzo beans), drained, rinsed
- 1 tablespoon rice bran oil
- 2 teaspoons ground cumin
- 2 teaspoons ground coriander
- 300g (9½ ounces) fresh ricotta
- large pinch each dried chilli flakes and oregano
- 300g (9½ ounces) vine-ripened baby cherry truss tomatoes
- ⅓ cup (35g) coarsely chopped walnuts
- ¼ cup fresh flat-leaf parsley leaves, torn

1 Preheat oven to 200°C/400°F. Line an oven tray with baking paper.

2 Place carrot, kumara, onion, capsicum and chickpeas on tray. Drizzle with half the oil and sprinkle with cumin and coriander. Toss gently to combine.

3 Place ricotta on tray alongside vegetables. Drizzle with remaining oil; sprinkle with chilli and oregano. Bake ricotta and vegetables for 40 minutes or until vegetables are tender, adding tomatoes to tray for the last 10 minutes of cooking time.

4 Serve vegetables and ricotta, topped with walnuts and parsley.

EGG FREE
GLUTEN FREE

**NUTRITIONAL
COUNT PER SERVING**
18.6g total fat
5.1g saturated fat
1672kJ (399 cal)
36g carbohydrate
16.8g protein
12.6g fibre

Dairy free
EGG FREE
GLUTEN FREE

**NUTRITIONAL
COUNT PER SERVING**
17.5g total fat
1.3g saturated fat
1756kJ (419 cal)
38.8g carbohydrate
14.7g protein
12.5g fibre

Tomato & fennel SOUP

PREP + COOK TIME 50 MINUTES SERVES 4

- 2 large fennel bulbs (1.1kg)
- 1 large kumara (orange sweet potato) (500g), cut into 2cm (¾-inch) pieces
- 4 medium tomatoes (600g), halved
- 1 large red onion (300g), cut into wedges
- 2 cloves garlic, unpeeled
- cooking-oil spray
- 1.25 litres (5 cups) gluten-free vegetable stock
- ⅔ cup (110g) natural almonds, chopped coarsely

1 Preheat oven to 200°C/400°F. Line a large oven tray with baking paper.

2 Trim fennel, reserving 1 tablespoon of fennel fronds; cut fennel into wedges. Combine fennel, kumara, tomato, onion and garlic on tray; spray with oil. Roast for 30 minutes or until tender and browned.

3 Peel garlic; blend or process kumara, tomato, fennel, onion, garlic and stock until smooth.

4 Pour soup into a medium saucepan; bring to the boil. Serve soup topped with almonds and reserved fronds.

Goat's cheese & fig jam
ROAST BEEF ON FLATBREAD

PREP + COOK TIME 1½ HOURS **SERVES** 4 (MAKES 10 FLATBREAD)

- 650g (1¼-pound) blade beef roast
- 1 teaspoon cracked black pepper
- 1 clove garlic, crushed
- 1 tablespoon finely grated lemon rind
- 2 tablespoons extra virgin olive oil
- 150g (4½-ounce) tub fig and walnut paste
- 50g (1½ ounces) baby rocket (arugula) leaves
- 100g (3 ounces) soft goat's cheese
- 1 lemon, zested

FLATBREAD

- 1½ cups (225g) 100% corn (maize) cornflour (cornstarch)
- 1½ cups (225g) buckwheat flour
- 2 eggs, beaten lightly
- 1 tablespoon extra virgin olive oil, plus 1 tablespoon extra
- ¾ cup (180ml) water, approximately

1 Preheat oven to 180°C/350°F.

2 Coat beef in combined pepper, garlic, rind and half the oil. Season. Place in an oiled baking tray. Roast for 50 minutes or until cooked as desired. Cover tightly with foil; rest for 10 minutes before carving.

3 Meanwhile, make flatbread.

4 To serve, spread four flatbread with paste, top with rocket, beef and crumbled cheese. Drizzle with remaining oil and sprinkle with zest, to serve. Season. Top with micro herbs, if you like.

flatbread Combine dry ingredients in a medium bowl; make a well in the centre. Add egg, oil and enough water to form a soft dough. Knead on a floured surface until smooth. Divide dough into 10 portions; roll each portion into a 3mm (⅛-inch) thick, 20cm (8-inch) oval. Brush with extra oil; cook on a heated grill pan (or barbecue) for 3 minutes each side or until browned and crisp.

TIPS

Wrap remaining flatbreads in plastic wrap and freeze for up to 3 months. These are also great to use as pizza bases.

NUT FREE
GLUTEN FREE
YEAST FREE

**NUTRITIONAL
COUNT PER SERVING**
38g total fat
13g saturated fat
4492kJ (1073 cal)
111g carbohydrate
66.6g protein
1.5g fibre

NUTRITIONAL COUNT PER SERVING
21.6g total fat
5.9g saturated fat
2422kJ (579 cal)
57.4g carbohydrate
34.3g protein
6.9g fibre

TURKEY & BROWN RICE SALAD

PREP + COOK TIME 40 MINUTES SERVES 4

- 1⅓ cups (260g) brown rice
- 200g (6 ounces) green beans, trimmed, halved lengthways
- 400g (12½ ounces) turkey breast steaks
- 6 red radishes (210g), sliced thinly
- 2 lebanese cucumbers (260g), halved, sliced thinly
- 80g (3 ounces) goat's cheese, crumbled
- 4 green onions (scallions), sliced thinly
- 2 trimmed celery stalks (200g), sliced thinly
- 2 tablespoons cashews, toasted, chopped coarsely
- 100g (3 ounces) baby rocket (arugula) leaves
- ½ cup loosely packed torn fresh basil leaves
- 2 tablespoons olive oil
- ⅓ cup (80ml) lemon juice

1 Place rice in a medium saucepan, cover with water; bring to the boil. Reduce heat; simmer, uncovered, for 35 minutes or until tender. Drain; rinse under cold water. Drain well.

2 Meanwhile, cook beans in a small saucepan of boiling water for 3 minutes or until just tender. Drain; refresh under cold water, drain.

3 Cook turkey on a heated oiled grill pan (or grill or barbecue) for 3 minutes each side or until cooked through. Cover; rest for 5 minutes, then slice thickly.

4 Place rice, beans and turkey in a large bowl with remaining ingredients; toss gently to combine.

TIPS

This recipe is perfect for any lunchbox as you can make it the night before; store, covered, in the fridge. If you're short on time, try making this salad with quinoa instead of rice; it will take less than half the time to cook and has a great fibre content, just like brown rice. You could use chicken breast or lamb fillets instead of the turkey.

Fennel, apple & pistachio
CHICKEN SALAD

PREP + COOK TIME 25 MINUTES (+ COOLING) **SERVES** 4

When poaching chicken, the secret to keeping it tender and moist, is to finish off the cooking in the gentle residual heat of the pan. This method also works well with fish.

- 2 cups (500ml) gluten-free chicken stock
- 2 cups (500ml) water
- 4 thin slices lemon
- 4 cloves garlic, bruised (see tips)
- 6 fresh thyme sprigs
- 2 x 200g (6½-ounce) free-range chicken breasts
- ½ cup (125ml) lemon juice
- 1 tablespoon dijon mustard
- ⅓ cup (80ml) extra virgin olive oil
- 1 small fennel (130g), sliced thinly
- 1 medium apple (150g), sliced thinly
- 1 cup (40g) trimmed watercress
- 1 cup firmly packed fresh flat-leaf parsley leaves
- 1 cup firmly packed torn fresh mint
- 1 medium avocado (250g), sliced thinly
- ½ cup (60g) pistachios, chopped coarsely

1 Place stock, the water, lemon slices, garlic and thyme in a medium saucepan over medium heat. Add chicken; bring to the boil. Reduce heat; simmer, uncovered, for 4 minutes. Cover pan, remove from heat; cool chicken in poaching liquid to room temperature. Remove chicken; shred coarsely. Reserve poaching liquid for another use (see tips).

2 Whisk juice and mustard in a small bowl until combined; gradually whisk in oil until combined. Season to taste.

3 Combine fennel, apple, watercress, herbs and avocado in a large bowl. Add chicken and dressing; toss to combine. Season to taste. Serve salad topped with pistachios.

TIPS

To bruise garlic, place the flat side of a cook's knife on the unpeeled clove; using the heel of your other hand push down on the knife to flatten it. Remove the skin. Store the reserved poaching liquid in the fridge for up to 3 days. Simply omit the pistachios to also make this salad nut free.

Dairy free
EGG FREE
GLUTEN FREE

**NUTRITIONAL
COUNT PER SERVING**
41.7g total fat
7.7g saturated fat
2268kJ (542 cal)
11g carbohydrate
28g protein
7.2g fibre

Dairy free
EGG FREE
GLUTEN FREE

**NUTRITIONAL
COUNT PER SERVING**
19g total fat
2.6g saturated fat
1904kJ (455 cal)
41.3g carbohydrate
28.3g protein
7g fibre

Wombok & herb salad with
BEEF & TAMARIND DRESSING

PREP + COOK TIME 15 MINUTES SERVES 4

- 1 tablespoon vegetable oil
- 300g (9½ ounces) beef stir-fry strips
- ½ small wombok (napa cabbage) (350g), shredded finely
- 1 fresh long red chilli, sliced thinly
- ¾ cup (105g) roasted peanuts, chopped coarsely
- 100g (3 ounces) baby spinach leaves
- 1½ cups loosely packed fresh mint leaves
- ½ cup loosely packed fresh vietnamese mint leaves

TAMARIND DRESSING

- 1½ tablespoons tamarind puree
- ½ cup (175g) brown rice syrup (see tips)
- 2 tablespoons lime juice
- 2 tablespoons fish sauce

1 Make tamarind dressing.

2 Heat oil in a wok over high heat; stir-fry beef strips for 3 minutes or until cooked through.

3 Place beef in a large bowl with wombok, chilli, peanuts, spinach, herbs and dressing; toss gently to combine.

tamarind dressing Whisk ingredients in a small bowl until combined.

TIPS

Brown rice syrup is also known as rice syrup or rice malt. It is available in the health food section of most supermarkets. Use prawns, chicken or tofu instead of the beef.

Chicken, almond &
SPINACH WRAPS

PREP + COOK TIME 25 MINUTES (+ COOLING) SERVES 4

- 2 x 200g (6½-ounce) chicken breast fillets
- 1 litre (4 cups) water
- ⅓ cup (100g) gluten-free whole-egg mayonnaise
- 1 tablespoon wholegrain mustard
- 1 tablespoon finely chopped fresh chives
- ½ cup (70g) slivered almonds
- 4 gluten-free wraps (250g)
- 80g (2½ ounces) curly endive leaves

1 Place chicken and the water in a medium saucepan over high heat; bring to the boil. Reduce heat to low; simmer, uncovered, for 10 minutes. Remove pan from heat; leave chicken in poaching liquid until completely cool.

2 Remove chicken from poaching liquid; shred coarsely. Discard liquid.

3 Place chicken in a large bowl with mayonnaise, mustard, chives and almonds; stir to combine. Season.

4 Place wraps in microwave oven; cook on HIGH (100%) in 5-second intervals until warm and pliable.

5 Divide chicken evenly among wraps; top with endive. Roll up to enclose filling.

TIPS

Use left over roast chicken or gluten-free barbecued chicken. Chicken mixture can be made up 2 days ahead; store, covered, in the refrigerator.

Dairy free
GLUTEN FREE

**NUTRITIONAL
COUNT PER SERVING**
39g total fat
6.1g saturated fat
2696kJ (645 cal)
44.4g carbohydrate
28.1g protein
0.7g fibre

EGG FREE

GLUTEN FREE

**NUTRITIONAL
COUNT PER SERVING**
16.6g total fat
2.7g saturated fat
1674kJ (400 cal)
31.4g carbohydrate
25.9g protein
14g fibre

Roasted brussels sprouts
& LENTIL SALAD

PREP + COOK TIME 1½ HOURS **SERVES** 4

- 1½ cup (300g) dried french-style green lentils
- 3 cups (750ml) water
- 16 brussels sprouts, trimmed, halved
- olive-oil spray
- ⅓ cup (45g) slivered almonds, toasted
- ½ cup fresh mint leaves
- ¼ cup (60ml) balsamic vinaigrette
- ⅓ cup (25g) shaved parmesan

1 Place lentils and the water in a small saucepan, bring to the boil over high heat. Reduce heat to low; simmer, covered, for 45 minutes or until lentils are tender. Drain.

2 Preheat oven to 200°C/400°F. Line an oven tray with baking paper.

3 Cook sprouts in a medium saucepan of boiling water, uncovered, for 3 minutes; drain. Spread sprouts on oven tray; spray with oil. Roast for 20 minutes or until golden.

4 Place lentils and sprouts in a large bowl with almonds, mint, vinaigrette and parmesan, season with pepper; toss gently to combine.

TIPS

If brussels sprouts aren't available use chopped cabbage. This salad is a great side for grilled chicken or fish.

Cauliflower PIZZA BITES

PREP + COOK TIME 45 MINUTES MAKES 24

- 300g (9½ ounces) cauliflower florets, chopped
- ½ cup (60g) ground almonds
- ¼ cup (30g) finely grated vintage cheddar
- 1 teaspoon finely chopped fresh rosemary
- 1 teaspoon finely chopped fresh oregano
- 1 egg, beaten lightly
- 2 lebanese eggplants (160g)
- 2 medium zucchini (240g)
- 1 tablespoon olive oil
- 1 cup (150g) canned crushed tomatoes
- 1 clove garlic, crushed
- 20g (¾ ounce) fetta, crumbled
- ¼ cup (40g) pine nuts, toasted
- 2 tablespoons fresh oregano leaves, extra

1 Preheat oven to 220°C/425°F. Grease two flat-based 12-hole (2-tablespoon/40ml) patty pan trays; line bases with small rounds of baking paper.

2 Pulse cauliflower in a food processor until it resembles fine crumbs; transfer to a large bowl. Add ground almonds, cheddar, herbs and egg; season and combine well. Spoon mixture into holes; press firmly on base and side to form a tart shell. Bake for 10 minutes or until golden and crisp. Leave oven on.

3 Meanwhile, use a mandoline or V-slicer to cut eggplant and zucchini into 3mm (⅛-inch) thick slices. Cook vegetables on a heated oiled grill plate (or grill), on one side only, for 2 minutes or until lightly charred. Transfer to a medium bowl, add oil and season; toss to coat.

4 Combine tomatoes and garlic in a small bowl. Spoon 1 teaspoon tomato mixture into each tart shell; top with grilled vegetables and fetta.

5 Bake bites for 5 minutes or until fetta is golden. Loosen each pizza bite from the pan using a butter knife. Serve topped with extra pine nuts and oregano.

TIPS

You can use any leftover cheese you have in the fridge instead of cheddar. Make a double batch of bases; freeze half so you have them at the ready. Pizza bites can be made a day ahead and reheated in the microwave, on a plate lined with paper towel, on HIGH (100%) for 1 minute. Stand 2 minutes before serving.

NUTRITIONAL COUNT PER BITE
4.2g total fat
0.7g saturated fat
214kJ (51 cal)
0.9g carbohydrate
1.9g protein
1g fibre

Dairy free
NUT FREE
GLUTEN FREE

**NUTRITIONAL
COUNT PER SLICE**
16.1g total fat
2.4g saturated fat
1400kJ (335 cal)
43.8g carbohydrate
3g protein
0.7g fibre

GLUTEN-FREE BREAD

PREP + COOK TIME 1½ HOURS (+ STANDING) **MAKES** 1 LOAF (12 SLICES)

- 3 cups (405g) gluten-free plain (all-purpose) flour
- ½ cup (75g) potato flour
- ½ cup (80g) brown rice flour
- ½ cup (80g) white rice flour
- 3 teaspoons (10g) dried yeast
- 2 teaspoons salt
- 2 teaspoons xanthan gum
- 1 egg
- 3 egg whites
- ¾ cup (180ml) olive oil
- 1 teaspoon vinegar
- 2 cups (500ml) warm water
- 1 tablespoon olive oil, extra
- 2 teaspoons salt, extra

1 Grease a 12cm x 20cm (4¾-inch x 8-inch) loaf pan; lightly dust with rice flour.

2 Combine sifted flours, yeast, salt and gum in a large bowl.

3 Place egg, egg whites, oil, vinegar and 1½ cups of the water in a large bowl of an electric mixer; beat on medium speed for 3½ minutes. Add remaining water and the flour mixture, 1 cup at a time, beating until mixture is combined and smooth.

4 Spoon mixture into loaf pan; smooth the surface. Cover; stand in a warm place for 45 minutes.

5 Preheat oven to 220°C/425°F.

6 Drizzle loaf with extra oil and sprinkle with extra salt. Bake for 1 hour or until crust is firm and golden brown and the loaf sounds hollow when tapped. Stand bread in pan for 5 minutes before turning, top-side up, onto a wire rack to cool. Serve with dairy-free spread, if you like.

TIPS

This bread is best eaten the day it is baked, however, it's great for toast or toasted sandwiches the next day. This mixture will make 6 gluten-free bread rolls - divide dough into 6 even portions, roll into balls and place on a greased and floured oven tray, stand 45 minutes. Drizzle rolls with oil and sprinkle with salt; bake for 30 minutes.

4 ways with
GLUTEN-FREE BREAD

NUT FREE
GLUTEN FREE

NUTRITIONAL COUNT PER ROLL
36.7g total fat
10.9g saturated fat
2750kJ (657 cal)
65.5g carbohydrate
15.1g protein
0.7g fibre

Dairy free
NUT FREE
GLUTEN FREE

NUTRITIONAL COUNT PER SLICE
19.9g total fat
3.3g saturated fat
1610kJ (385 cal)
45.8g carbohydrate
4.5g protein
1.2g fibre

ONION & OLIVE BREAD

**PREP + COOK TIME 1 HOUR 50 MINUTES
(+ STANDING) MAKES 1 LOAF (12 SLICES)**

Heat 1 tablespoon olive oil in a large frying pan; cook 2 large (400g) thinly sliced brown onions over low heat for 10 minutes, stirring frequently until softened and golden in colour. Cut 1 cup (150g) seeded drained kalamata olives in half. Combine olives with onion; cool. Meanwhile, make gluten-free bread on page 97, to the end of step 3. Add onion mixture; fold through dough. Continue following recipe to the end of Step 6. Serve warm.

**TIPS This bread is best eaten on the day it is made.
Bread can be cut into slices or pulled apart for eating.
Freeze bread for up to 3 months.**

CHEESE & BACON ROLLS

**PREP + COOK TIME 1 HOUR 50 MINUTES
(+ STANDING) MAKES 8 ROLLS**

Finely chop 4 rindless bacon slices (250g) and coarsely grate 150g (4½oz) cheddar cheese. Make gluten-free bread on page 97 following steps 2 and 3. Add half the bacon and half the cheese; fold through dough. Divide dough into 8 portions. With wet hands, roll portions into balls. Place on an oiled and baking-paper-lined oven tray; sprinkle with remaining bacon and cheese. Cover rolls, stand in a warm place for 45 minutes. Preheat oven to 220°C/425°F. Bake for 40 minutes or until golden in colour and rolls sound hollow when tapped. Stand rolls on tray for 5 minutes before transferring to a wire rack to cool. Serve warm.

**TIPS If cheese starts to become too brown, cover with foil.
These rolls are best eaten on the day they are baked.
Freeze rolls for up to 3 months. Microwave cold rolls in
10-second bursts until heated through.**

**NUTRITIONAL
COUNT PER ROLL**
29.8g total fat
7.8g saturated fat
2430kJ (580 cal)
65.7g carbohydrate
10.8g protein
1.2g fibre

Dairy free
NUT FREE
GLUTEN FREE

NUT FREE
GLUTEN FREE

**NUTRITIONAL
COUNT PER SLICE**
24.5g total fat
3.8g saturated fat
1848kJ (441 cal)
45.8g carbohydrate
8.1g protein
1.2g fibre

SPINACH & FETTA ROLLS

**PREP + COOK TIME 1 HOUR 50 MINUTES
(+ STANDING) MAKES 8 ROLLS**

Wash and trim 1 bunch (500g) spinach; place in a heatproof bowl. Pour boiling water over spinach, stand 1 minute; drain. Rinse under cold water, drain; squeeze excess water from spinach. Roughly chop. Make gluten-free bread on page 97 following steps 2 and 3. Add spinach and 200g (6½oz) crumbled fetta; fold through dough. Divide dough into 8 portions. With wet hands, roll portions into balls. Place on an oiled and baking-paper-lined oven tray. Cover, stand in a warm place for 45 minutes. Preheat oven to 220°C/425°F. Bake for 40 minutes or until golden in colour and rolls sound hollow when tapped. Stand rolls on tray for 5 minutes before transferring to a wire rack to cool. Serve warm.

**TIPS These rolls are best eaten on the day they are made.
Freeze for up to 3 months. Microwave cold rolls in 10-second
bursts until heated through.**

4 SEED LOAF

**PREP + COOK TIME 1 HOUR 50 MINUTES
(+ STANDING) MAKES 1 LOAF (12 SLICES)**

Make gluten-free bread on page 97 to the end of step 3. Add ½ cup pepitas (pumpkin seed kernels), ⅓ cup each sunflower seeds and linseeds, and 2 tablespoons white chia seeds; fold through dough until combined. Spoon mixture into loaf pan; level the surface. Sprinkle with 2 teaspoons each pepitas (pumpkin seed kernels), sunflower seeds, linseeds and chia seeds; gently press into dough. Continue following recipe to the end of Step 6, omitting salt. Serve warm.

**TIPS This bread is best eaten on the day it is made.
Bread can be cut into slices and frozen for up to 3 months.**

Dinner

Gluten-free fettuccine
WITH ARRABBIATA SAUCE

PREP + COOK TIME 1 HOUR SERVES 4

- ½ cup (90g) white rice flour, plus extra for dusting
- ¼ cup (45g) sweet white sorghum flour
- ⅓ cup (50g) potato flour
- 1 tablespoon 100% corn (maize) cornflour (cornstarch)
- 2 teaspoons xanthan gum
- ¼ teaspoon sea salt
- 3 eggs
- 1 tablespoon olive oil
- shaved parmesan, to serve (optional) (see tips)

ARRABBIATA SAUCE

- 1 tablespoon olive oil
- 1 medium brown onion (150g), chopped finely
- 2 cloves garlic, crushed
- 3 fresh small red chillies, chopped finely
- 2 x 400g (12½-ounce) cans cherry tomatoes
- 1 tablespoon balsamic vinegar

1 Process flours, gum, salt, eggs and oil until ingredients form a dough. Turn out onto a surface dusted with extra rice flour; knead for 5 minutes or until smooth.

2 Divide dough into four. Wrap three pieces in plastic wrap until ready to use. Roll one piece on floured surface until thin enough to fit through the thickest setting on a pasta machine. Roll dough through thickest setting, dusting with rice flour when needed. Repeat.

3 Reduce the settings on pasta machine, rolling dough through each setting twice until dough is 2mm thick (second last setting on machine). Cover pasta sheets with a damp clean tea towel. Repeat with remaining dough.

4 To make fettuccine, use the fettuccine setting on pasta machine, carefully feed pasta sheets through the machine dusting with rice flour as needed. Place pasta under damp tea towel until ready to cook.

5 Meanwhile, make arrabbiata sauce.

6 Cook pasta in a large saucepan of salted boiling water about 1 minute or until just tender. Drain.

7 Serve pasta with sauce, topped with shaved parmesan and fresh basil leaves, if you like.

arrabbiata sauce Heat oil in medium saucepan over medium heat; cook, onion, garlic and chilli, for 5 minutes or until onion is soft. Add tomatoes and vinegar; cook over low heat, stirring occasionally, for 5 minutes or until sauce has thickened slightly and is heated through.

TIPS

Pasta can be made a day ahead; store, covered, in the fridge. Cooked pasta can be frozen for up to 3 months; refresh under hot water. Use packaged gluten-free pasta instead, if you like. This recipe is also dairy-free if served without the parmesan.

NUT FREE
GLUTEN FREE

NUTRITIONAL
COUNT PER SERVING
12.8g total fat
2.6g saturated fat
1455kJ (348 cal)
46.8g carbohydrate
8.8g protein
5.8g fibre

**NUTRITIONAL
COUNT PER SERVING**
39g total fat
13.8g saturated fat
2754kJ (658 cal)
30.3g carbohydrate
45g protein
4.3g fibre

Tomato & spinach
STUFFED LAMB ROASTS

PREP + COOK TIME 35 MINUTES **SERVES** 4

- ½ cup (75g) drained, coarsely chopped sun-dried tomatoes
- 100g (3 ounces) fetta, crumbled
- 40g (1½ ounces) baby spinach leaves, chopped coarsely
- 2 mini lamb roasts (700g)
- 800g (1½ pounds) kumara (orange sweet potato), cut into wedges
- 2 tablespoons olive oil
- 6 sprigs fresh thyme
- ¼ teaspoon dried chilli flakes

1 Preheat oven to 200°C/400°F.

2 Combine tomato, fetta and spinach in a medium bowl.

3 Cut a horizontal pocket in each roast; do not cut all the way through. Press half the tomato mixture into each pocket; secure with toothpicks.

4 Heat an oiled large ovenproof frying pan over high heat; cook lamb roasts, turning, until browned all over.

5 Meanwhile, place kumara in a roasting pan, drizzle with oil and sprinkle with thyme and chilli; toss to coat. Season.

6 Place frying pan and roasting pan in oven; roast, uncovered, for 20 minutes or until lamb is cooked as desired and kumara is golden and tender. Cover lamb; rest for 10 minutes.

7 Serve lamb sliced with kumara wedges.

TIPS

The lamb mini roasts are best stuffed just before roasting. Prepare the tomato and spinach filling ahead of time; store, covered, in the fridge until ready to use.

Lemon garlic lamb kebabs
WITH GREEK SALAD

PREP + COOK TIME 30 MINUTES **SERVES** 4

- 8 x 15cm (6-inch) stalks fresh rosemary
- 800g (1½ pounds) lamb fillets, cut into 3cm (1¼-inch) pieces
- 3 cloves garlic, crushed
- 2 tablespoons olive oil
- 2 teaspoons finely grated lemon rind
- 1 tablespoon lemon juice

GREEK SALAD

- 375g (12 ounces) baby roma (egg) tomatoes, halved, cut into wedges
- 2 lebanese cucumbers (260g), halved lengthways, sliced thinly
- 1 medium red capsicum (bell pepper) (200g), chopped coarsely
- 1 medium red onion (170g), sliced thinly
- ¼ cup (40g) pitted black olives
- 200g (6½ ounces) fetta, crumbled coarsely
- 2 teaspoons small fresh oregano leaves
- ¼ cup (60ml) extra virgin olive oil
- 2 tablespoons cider vinegar

1 Remove leaves from the bottom two-thirds of each rosemary stalk; sharpen trimmed ends into a point.

2 Thread lamb onto rosemary skewers; brush with combined garlic, oil, rind and juice. Cover; refrigerate until required.

3 Make greek salad.

4 Cook kebabs on a heated oiled grill plate (or grill or barbecue) for 10 minutes, turning and brushing with remaining garlic mixture, until cooked.

5 Serve kebabs with greek salad.

greek salad Combine ingredients in a large bowl.

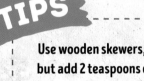

TIPS

Use wooden skewers, if you prefer, but add 2 teaspoons chopped fresh rosemary to garlic mixture.

Egg free
NUT FREE
GLUTEN FREE

**NUTRITIONAL
COUNT PER SERVING**
48.2g total fat
15.4g saturated fat
2920kJ (698 cal)
8.2g carbohydrate
55.3g protein
4.7g fibre

Egg free
NUT FREE
GLUTEN FREE

**NUTRITIONAL
COUNT PER SERVING**
50.7g total fat
9.5g saturated fat
2629kJ (629 cal)
15.8g carbohydrate
23.1g protein
12.6g fibre

Seeded CAULIFLOWER FALAFEL

PREP + COOK TIME 1 HOUR SERVES 6 (MAKES 30 FALAFEL)

- ½ cup (100g) pepitas (pumpkin seed kernels)
- ½ cup (75g) sunflower seed kernels
- ¼ cup (35g) sesame seeds
- 2 tablespoons linseeds (flaxseeds)
- 700g (1½ pounds) cauliflower, cut into florets
- 2 cloves garlic, crushed
- 1½ tablespoons cumin seeds, crushed
- 1½ tablespoons coriander seeds, crushed
- ½ cup loosely packed fresh mint leaves
- ½ cup loosely packed fresh flat-leaf parsley leaves
- ½ cup (140g) tahini
- 2 tablespoons psyllium husks (see tips)
- 2 tablespoons lemon juice
- ¼ cup (60ml) water
- rice bran oil, for deep-frying

SALAD

- 1 small red onion (100g), sliced thinly into rings
- 250g (8 ounces) grape tomatoes, sliced crossways
- ¼ cup (60ml) red wine vinegar
- 140g (4½ ounces) persian fetta

HUMMUS

- 400g (12½ ounces) canned chickpeas (garbanzo beans), undrained
- ¼ cup (70g) tahini
- 1 clove garlic
- 1½ tablespoons lemon juice
- 1 teaspoon cumin seeds, crushed

1 Make salad and hummus.

2 Heat a medium frying pan over medium-high heat, add pepitas, sunflower seeds, sesame seeds and linseeds; cook, stirring, for 2 minutes or until sesame seeds are golden.

3 Process toasted seeds with cauliflower and remaining ingredients (except rice bran oil) to a coarse paste; season well. Line an oven tray with baking paper. Using a dessert spoon, scoop up a mound of mixture. Hold a second dessert spoon the same size upside down and drag it over the falafel mixture in an arc shape as you reach the other side, bring the top of the spoon under the scoop of falafel mixture transferring it onto it in the process. Using the first spoon, push the quenelle-shaped falafel onto the tray.

4 Fill a medium saucepan two-thirds full with oil, heat to 160°C/325°F (or until oil sizzles when a small cube of bread is added). Fry, six falafel at a time, for 5 minutes or until dark golden and cooked through. Drain on paper towel.

5 Spoon hummus onto plates, top with falafel and salad. If you like, sprinkle with extra mint and parsley leaves.

salad Place onion, tomato and vinegar in a small bowl; stand for 30 minutes. Stir in fetta.

hummus Process chickpeas and canning liquid with remaining ingredients for 3 minutes or until smooth.

TIPS

Psyllium husks are obtained from the seeds of a plant native to India. They are useful for their binding qualities and are a good source of dietary fibre. Buy at vitamin and health food shops. Crushing whole spices in a pestle and mortar yourself adds a greater depth of flavour than you'd get from using the ready ground version of the same spice.

Pork fillet with
APPLE & LEEK

PREP + COOK TIME 35 MINUTES **SERVES** 4

- 800g (1½ pounds) pork fillets
- ¾ cup (180ml) gluten-free chicken stock
- 2 medium leeks (700g), sliced thickly
- 1 clove garlic, crushed
- 2 tablespoons brown sugar
- 2 tablespoons red wine vinegar
- 10g (½ ounce) butter
- 2 medium apples (300g), unpeeled, sliced thinly
- 1 tablespoon brown sugar, extra
- 400g (12½ ounces) baby carrots, trimmed
- 250g (8 ounces) asparagus, trimmed, chopped coarsely

1 Preheat oven to 240°C/475°F.

2 Cook pork in a heated oiled frying pan, over medium-high heat, until browned all over. Place, in a single layer, in a large baking dish; bake, uncovered, for 20 minutes or until pork is cooked as desired. Cover; stand 5 minutes before slicing thickly.

3 Meanwhile, heat half the stock in a medium frying pan over medium-high heat; cook leek and garlic, stirring, for 10 minutes or until leek softens and browns slightly. Add sugar and vinegar; cook, stirring, for 5 minutes or until leek caramelises.

4 Add remaining stock to pan; bring to the boil. Reduce heat; simmer, uncovered, for 5 minutes or until liquid reduces by half. Place leek mixture in a medium bowl; cover to keep warm.

5 Melt butter in same pan over medium heat; cook apple and extra sugar, stirring, for 5 minutes or until apple is browned and tender.

6 Boil, steam or microwave carrot and asparagus, separately, until just tender; drain.

7 Serve pork with vegetables, caramelised apple and leek; season to taste.

TIPS

Pork has a natural affinity with both apple and onion; here, these traditional accompaniments are given a contemporary twist. Serve pork with any steamed vegetable that is in season. The leek mixture can be made several hours ahead; store, covered, in the fridge. Reheat before serving.

Egg free
NUT FREE
GLUTEN FREE

NUTRITIONAL
COUNT PER SERVING
7.3g total fat
3.1g saturated fat
1635kJ (391 cal)
28.1g carbohydrate
48.5g protein
9.7g fibre

Dairy free
EGG FREE
GLUTEN FREE

**NUTRITIONAL
COUNT PER SERVING**
36.1g total fat
10.9g saturated fat
2515kJ (601 cal)
16.9g carbohydrate
48.7g protein
5.2g fibre

Five-spice beef
WITH ALMONDS

PREP + COOK TIME 35 MINUTES **SERVES** 4

- 750g (1½-pound) piece beef eye-fillet, sliced thinly
- 1 teaspoon garam masala
- 2 teaspoons chinese five-spice powder
- 1 tablespoon peanut oil
- 1 medium carrot (120g), cut into long thin strips
- 1 large red capsicum (bell pepper) (350g), cut into long thin strips
- 2 cloves garlic, crushed
- 1 tablespoon finely grated fresh ginger
- 170g (5½ ounces) coarsely chopped choy sum
- 3 teaspoons sambal oelek
- 2 tablespoons gluten-free oyster sauce
- 2 tablespoons mango chutney
- 2 tablespoons lime juice
- 2 tablespoons water
- 100g (3 ounces) snow peas, trimmed
- 1 cup (80g) bean sprouts
- ⅓ cup (55g) blanched almonds, toasted, chopped coarsely

1 Combine beef and spices in a large bowl.

2 Heat half the oil in a wok over high heat; stir-fry beef mixture, in batches, for 3 minutes or until beef is browned and tender. Remove from wok.

3 Heat remaining oil in wok; stir-fry carrot, capsicum, garlic and ginger for 2 minutes. Add choy sum, sambal, sauce, chutney, juice and the water; stir-fry for 4 minutes or until choy sum is tender.

4 Return beef to wok with snow peas and sprouts; stir-fry until heated through. Serve topped with almonds.

TIPS

You can substitute beef with chicken or pork. Replace the peanut oil with vegetable oil and omit the almonds to make this recipe nut-free.

Olive chicken with
MAPLE ROASTED VEGETABLES

PREP + COOK TIME 1 HOUR 50 MINUTES **SERVES** 4

- ¼ cup (60ml) olive oil
- 1 whole chicken (1.6kg), cut into 10 pieces
- 1 medium brown onion (150g), chopped coarsely
- 2 cloves garlic, crushed
- 3 sprigs fresh thyme
- 18 sicilian green olives (90g)
- 1 litre (4 cups) gluten-free chicken stock
- 1 tablespoon lemon juice

MAPLE ROASTED VEGETABLES

- 600g (1¼ pounds) kent pumpkin, cut into 2cm (¾-inch) wedges
- 4 small parsnips (480g), unpeeled, quartered lengthways
- 400g (12½ ounces) spring onions, trimmed to 10cm (4-inch) lengths, quartered lengthways
- 2 tablespoons extra virgin olive oil
- 2 tablespoons pure maple syrup
- 1 cup (40g) loosely packed rocket (arugula) leaves
- 1 tablespoon lemon juice

1 Heat oil in a large heavy-based saucepan over high heat; cook chicken, in batches, for 2 minutes each side or until browned. Remove from pan.

2 Reduce heat of same pan to medium; cook onion, garlic, thyme and olives, stirring occasionally, for 5 minutes or until onion is softened. Increase heat to high; return chicken and any juices to pan. Add stock; bring to the boil. Reduce heat to low; simmer, covered, for 1 hour or until chicken is cooked through. Remove chicken from pan.

3 Meanwhile, preheat oven to 200°C/400°F; make maple roasted vegetables.

4 Increase saucepan heat to high; bring to the boil. Reduce heat slightly; cook, uncovered, for 20 minutes or until liquid has reduced to 1 cup (250ml). Add juice, season to taste.

5 Serve chicken with reduced mixture and vegetables.

maple roasted vegetables Line two oven trays with baking paper. Divide pumpkin, parsnip and onion between trays; drizzle with oil and maple syrup, season, then toss to coat. Roast for 40 minutes, turning halfway through cooking or until vegetables are tender. Combine rocket and lemon juice in a medium bowl; season to taste. Just before serving, toss rocket through vegetables.

TIPS

These olives contain pits, so warn your guests before eating. Alternatively use pitted olives.

Dairy free
NUT FREE
GLUTEN FREE
EGG FREE

**NUTRITIONAL
COUNT PER SERVING**
57.1g total fat
13.1g saturated fat
3758kJ (899 cal)
36.3g carbohydrate
57g protein
10g fibre

Beef & vegetable pot pies
WITH KUMARA TOPPING

PREP + COOK TIME 2¼ HOURS (+ COOLING) **SERVES** 4

- 1 tablespoon olive oil
- 800g (1½-pound) beef blade steak,
  cut into 2cm (¾-inch) pieces
- 2 medium brown onions (300g), chopped finely
- 2 medium carrots (240g), sliced thinly
- 2 trimmed celery stalks (200g), sliced thinly
- 2 cloves garlic, crushed
- 1 cup (250ml) dry red wine
- 2 cups (500ml) gluten-free beef stock
- 2 tablespoons 100% corn (maize) cornflour (cornstarch)
- 2 tablespoons water
- 2 tablespoons coarsely chopped fresh oregano

KUMARA TOPPING
- 750g (1½ pounds) kumara (orange sweet potato),
  peeled, chopped coarsely
- 100g (2½ ounces) soft goat's cheese

1 Heat oil in a medium saucepan over high heat; cook beef, in batches, stirring, for 2 minutes or until browned. Remove from pan.

2 Reduce heat to medium; cook onion, carrot, celery and garlic in same pan, stirring, for 5 minutes or until vegetables have softened. Return beef to pan with combined wine and beef stock; bring to the boil. Reduce heat to low; simmer, uncovered, stirring occasionally, for 1½ hours or until beef is tender and sauce thickens.

3 Meanwhile, make kumara topping.

4 Combine cornflour and the water; add to beef mixture. Cook, stirring, over high heat, for 5 minutes or until sauce boils and thickens. Season; cool. Stir in oregano.

5 Preheat oven to 200°C/400°F. Oil four 10cm (4-inch), 1 cup (250ml) ovenproof dishes; place on baking tray.

6 Spoon beef mixture into dishes, top with kumara topping. Bake for 30 minutes or until filling is hot. Sprinkle with extra oregano, if you like.

kumara topping Boil, steam or microwave kumara until soft. Combine kumara with goat's cheese in a small bowl.

TIPS

Swap kumara for potato or pumpkin, if you like.
Pies can be frozen for up to 3 months.

Chilli lime snapper with
CORN SALSA SALAD

PREP + COOK TIME 35 MINUTES SERVES 4

- ¼ cup (60ml) olive oil
- 1 clove garlic, sliced thinly
- 1 fresh long green chilli, seeded, chopped finely
- 1 teaspoon finely grated lime rind
- 4 x 180g (5½-ounce) boneless, skinless snapper fillets
- 2 corn cobs (250g), husks removed
- 6 red radishes (90g), sliced thinly
- 45g (1½ ounces) snowpea sprouts, trimmed
- 1 green onion (scallion), sliced thinly
- ¼ cup fresh coriander (cilantro) leaves
- 1 tablespoon lime juice
- 1 tablespoon white balsamic vinegar or white vinegar
- 1 tablespoon olive oil, extra
- 1 medium avocado (250g), sliced
- lime wedges, to serve

1 Combine 2 tablespoons of the oil with garlic, chilli and rind in a small bowl; add snapper, turn to coat. Set aside.

2 Brush corn with remaining oil; cook on a heated grill plate (or barbecue), turning every 2 minutes, for 8 minutes or until corn is cooked and lightly charred. Cool.

3 Place radish, sprouts, green onion and coriander in a bowl of iced water to crisp.

4 Cut kernels from cooled cobs; place in a large bowl with juice, vinegar and extra oil. Remove radish mixture from water with a slotted spoon; drain on paper towel. Add to corn mixture, season to taste; toss gently to combine.

5 Line the grill plate with baking paper (ensure paper doesn't extend over the edge); cook snapper on heated plate, for 2 minutes each side or until just cooked through.

6 Serve snapper with corn salsa salad, avocado and lime.

TIPS

You can use any fish fillets you like or even prawns for this recipe.

**NUTRITIONAL
COUNT PER SERVING**
32.3g total fat
6g saturated fat
2465kJ (589 cal)
25.5g carbohydrate
44.5g protein
8.9g fibre

Egg free
NUT FREE
GLUTEN FREE

**NUTRITIONAL
COUNT PER SERVING**
37.3g total fat
9.3g saturated fat
2373kJ (567 cal)
4.5g carbohydrate
51.7g protein
2.9g fibre

Char-grilled cuttlefish,
ROCKET & PARMESAN SALAD

PREP + COOK TIME 30 MINUTES **SERVES** 4

- 1kg (2 pounds) cuttlefish hoods
- 2 tablespoons olive oil
- 1 tablespoon finely grated lemon rind
- ⅓ cup (80ml) lemon juice
- 1 clove garlic, crushed
- 150g (4½ ounces) rocket (arugula)
- 1 small radicchio (150g), leaves separated
- 200g (6½ ounces) yellow cherry tomatoes, halved
- 1 small red onion (100g), sliced thinly
- 1 tablespoon rinsed, drained baby capers
- 1 cup (80g) shaved parmesan
- 2 tablespoons balsamic vinegar
- ⅓ cup (80ml) olive oil, extra

1 Halve cuttlefish lengthways, score insides in a crosshatch pattern, then cut into 5cm (2-inch) strips. Place cuttlefish in a medium bowl with oil, rind, juice and garlic; stir well to combine. Cover; refrigerate for 10 minutes.

2 Meanwhile, place rocket, radicchio, tomato, onion, capers and parmesan in a large bowl; toss gently to combine.

3 Drain cuttlefish; discard marinade. Cook cuttlefish, in batches, on a heated oiled grill plate (or grill or barbecue) for 4 minutes or until browned and cooked through.

4 Add cuttlefish to salad with combined vinegar and the extra oil; toss gently to combine.

TIPS

You can use witlof or rocket instead of the radicchio.

Eggplant lasagne
WITH CASHEW CREAM

PREP + COOK TIME 2 HOURS (+ STANDING) **SERVES** 6

- 1 tablespoon olive oil
- 1 medium brown onion (150g), chopped finely
- 2 trimmed celery stalks (100g), chopped finely
- 1 medium carrot (120g), chopped finely
- 2 cloves garlic, crushed
- 1kg (2 pounds) minced (ground) beef
- 2 x 400g (12½-ounce) cans diced tomatoes
- ¼ cup (70g) tomato paste
- ½ cup (125ml) dry red wine
- ¼ cup shredded fresh basil leaves
- olive oil cooking spray
- 3 large eggplant (1.5kg), sliced thinly

CASHEW CREAM
- 2 cups (300g) raw cashews
- 1½ cups (375ml) water

1 Heat oil in a large frying pan over medium heat; cook onion, celery, carrot and garlic, stirring, for 5 minutes or until soft.

2 Add beef; cook, stirring, for 5 minutes or until changed in colour. Add tomatoes, paste and wine; bring to the boil. Reduce heat to low; simmer, uncovered, for 1 hour or until sauce is rich and thickened. Stir in basil; season.

3 Meanwhile, preheat grill (broiler) to hot. Spray eggplant with oil; place on a oiled baking tray. Grill eggplant, in batches, for 1-2 minutes each side or until lightly browned and tender. Set aside to cool.

4 Make cashew cream.

5 Preheat oven to 180°C/350°F. Oil a 19cm x 29cm (8-inch x 11¾-inch) baking dish. Place one-third of the beef sauce on base of dish. Top with one-third of the eggplant and spread with one-third of the cashew cream. Repeat layering finishing with cashew cream.

6 Bake lasagne for 40 minutes or until lightly browned and heated through. Stand for 5 minutes before serving.

cashew cream Place cashews in a large bowl, cover with cold water. Stand for 30 minutes; drain. Blend or process cashews with the water until smooth. Season.

TIPS

For a richer cashew cream you can use roasted cashews. You can swap the eggplant for zucchini. Lasagne can be frozen up to 3 months.

Dairy free
EGG FREE
GLUTEN FREE

**NUTRITIONAL
COUNT PER SERVING**
47.6g total fat
12.8g saturated fat
3271kJ (781 cal)
22.2g carbohydrate
57.8g protein
13.2g fibre

**NUTRITIONAL
COUNT PER SERVING**
20.5g total fat
9.7g saturated fat
1982kJ (474 cal)
14.6g carbohydrate
50.2g protein
7.6g fibre

Steak bourguignon with
CELERIAC POTATO MASH

PREP + COOK TIME 40 MINUTES SERVES 4

- 1 small celeriac (celery root) (400g), chopped coarsely
- 2 medium potatoes (400g), chopped coarsely
- 40g (1½ ounces) butter
- ¼ cup (60ml) milk
- cooking-oil spray
- 4 x 200g (6½-ounce) beef eye-fillet steaks
- 200g (6½ ounces) button mushrooms, halved
- 6 baby onions (150g), quartered
- 2 cloves garlic, crushed
- ½ cup (125ml) dry red wine
- 1 cup (250ml) gluten-free beef stock
- 1 tablespoon tomato paste
- 1 tablespoon coarsely chopped fresh thyme leaves

1 Boil, steam or microwave celeriac and potato, separately, until tender; drain. Mash celeriac and potato in a medium bowl with butter and milk. Cover to keep warm.

2 Meanwhile, spray a large frying pan with cooking oil; heat over medium-high heat. Cook beef for 4 minutes each side or until browned and cooked as desired. Remove from pan; cover to keep warm.

3 Cook mushrooms, onion and garlic in same pan until vegetables just soften. Add wine, stock and paste; simmer, uncovered, for 5 minutes or until sauce thickens slightly.

4 Serve beef with mash and bourguignon sauce; sprinkle with thyme. Serve with roasted heirloom carrots, if you like.

TIPS

Mash can be made a day ahead; store, covered, in the fridge. Reheat just before serving. You can substitute rib-eye (scotch fillet) or sirloin (new-york cut) steak for eye-fillet.

Lamb, haloumi & kale salad
WITH CHIMICHURRI DRESSING

PREP + COOK TIME 40 MINUTES **SERVES** 6

- 600g (1¼ pound) lamb rump steaks, trimmed
- 2 teaspoons olive oil
- 1 small red onion (120g), sliced thinly
- 2 cups (60g) thickly sliced kale leaves
- 250g (8 ounces) haloumi, sliced thickly
- 2 small tomatoes (180g), seeded, sliced thinly
- 200g (6½-ounce) packet crunchy combo of sprouts

CHIMICHURRI DRESSING

- 1 cup coarsely chopped fresh flat-leaf parsley
- 2 tablespoons coarsely chopped fresh oregano
- 2 cloves garlic, crushed
- 1 tablespoon red wine vinegar
- 2 tablespoons lemon juice
- ½ cup (125ml) extra virgin olive oil

1 Make chimichurri dressing.

2 Cook lamb on a heated, oiled grill pan (or grill or barbecue) for 4 minutes each side or until cooked as desired. Transfer to a plate; cover tightly with foil, rest for 5 minutes. Slice lamb into 5mm (¼-inch) slices.

3 Meanwhile, heat oil in a large frying pan; cook onion, stirring, for 5 minutes or until just softened. Add kale; cook, stirring, for 2 minutes until kale changes colour and softens slightly. Transfer to a large bowl.

4 Cook haloumi in same pan, over medium heat, for 1 minute each side or until browned and just melting.

5 Add lamb and haloumi to kale mixture, with tomato and sprouts; toss gently to combine. Serve salad drizzled with chimichurri dressing.

chimichurri dressing Combine ingredients in a bowl.

TIPS

Any leftover chimichurri can be stored in an airtight container in the fridge for up to 2 weeks.

**NUTRITIONAL
COUNT PER SERVING**
1.8g total fat
0.2g saturated fat
824kJ (196 cal)
4.9g carbohydrate
37.4g protein
3.4g fibre

Steamed fish &
VEGETABLE PARCELS

PREP + COOK TIME 35 MINUTES **SERVES** 4

- 2 medium carrots (240g), cut into matchsticks
- 2 medium zucchini (240g), cut into matchsticks
- 4 x 200g (6½-ounce) firm white fish fillets
- ⅓ cup (80ml) lemon juice
- 2 tablespoons fresh dill

1 Preheat oven to 200°C/400°F.

2 Divide carrots and zucchini equally between four 30cm (12-inch) squares of baking paper. Place fish on vegetables; drizzle with juice. Fold ends and sides of paper to enclose fish (secure parcel with kitchen string, if necessary).

3 Place parcels on an oven tray; bake for 15 minutes or until fish is just cooked.

4 Before serving, season fish and top with dill. Serve with roasted smashed potatoes, if you like.

TIPS

Any firm fish fillets can be used, such as red mullet, murray cod or queenfish.

Fish tortilla with
TOMATO & AVOCADO SALSA

PREP + COOK TIME 20 MINUTES SERVES 4

- 1 tablespoon smoked paprika
- ½ teaspoon cayenne powder
- 1 teaspoon ground cumin
- 12 flathead fillets (1.2kg)
- 1 tablespoon olive oil
- 312g (10-ounce) packet gluten-free white corn tortillas

TOMATO & AVOCADO SALSA

- 2 medium tomatoes (340g), seeded, chopped finely
- 1 large avocado (320g), chopped finely
- 1 small red onion (100g), sliced thinly
- ⅓ cup fresh coriander (cilantro) leaves

CHILLI LIME DRESSING

- 1 tablespoon lime juice
- 2 teaspoons caster (superfine) sugar
- 1 fresh small red thai (serrano) chilli, seeded, sliced thinly
- 1 tablespoon olive oil

1 Combine paprika, cayenne pepper and cumin in a small bowl; rub all over fish.

2 Heat oil in a medium frying pan over high heat; cook fish, in batches, for 5 minutes, turning occasionally or until cooked through. Remove from pan; cover to keep warm.

3 Wipe pan clean with paper towel. Heat pan over high heat; cook tortillas one at a time, for 30 seconds each side or until heated through. Remove from pan; cover with foil to keep warm.

4 Meanwhile, make tomato and avocado salsa, then chilli lime dressing.

5 Serve fish in tortillas with avocado mixture. Drizzle with dressing. Scatter with extra coriander leaves, if you like.

tomato & avocado salsa Place ingredients in a large bowl; toss gently to combine.

chilli lime dressing Combine ingredients in a small bowl.

TIPS

Any white fish fillets can be used in this recipe.

GLUTEN FREE

NUTRITIONAL COUNT PER SERVING
25.9g total fat
5.6g saturated fat
2826kJ (676 cal)
37.7g carbohydrate
69.3g protein
3.5g fibre

**NUTRITIONAL
COUNT PER SERVING**
12.5g total fat
5g saturated fat
2229kJ (533 cal)
37.1g carbohydrate
64g protein
5g fibre

Mustard veal with
POLENTA & SPINACH PUREE

PREP + COOK TIME 35 MINUTES SERVES 4

- ⅓ cup (95g) wholegrain mustard
- 2 tablespoons coarsely chopped fresh oregano
- 2 cloves garlic, crushed
- 8 veal chops (1.5kg)
- 350g (11 ounces) truss cherry tomatoes
- 2 cups (500ml) water
- 1 teaspoon salt
- 1 cup (170g) polenta
- ¾ cup (180ml) milk
- ¼ cup (20g) finely grated parmesan
- 350g (11 ounces) spinach, trimmed
- 2 cloves garlic, extra, crushed
- 1 anchovy fillet, drained
- 1 tablespoon lemon juice
- 1 cup (250ml) gluten-free beef stock

1 Place grill shelf on the low rung. Preheat grill (broiler) to medium-high heat.

2 Combine mustard, oregano and garlic in a small bowl; brush veal both sides with mixture. Cook veal under grill until browned both sides and cooked as desired. Remove from heat; cover to keep warm.

3 Preheat oven to 180°C/350°F.

4 Place tomatoes on a baking-paper-lined oven tray; roast in oven for 10 minutes or until softened.

5 Meanwhile, bring the water and salt to the boil in a medium saucepan. Stir in polenta, reduce heat to low; cook, stirring, for 10 minutes or until polenta thickens. Stir in milk; cook, stirring, for 5 minutes or until polenta thickens. Stir in parmesan; season to taste.

6 Boil, steam or microwave spinach until just wilted. When cool enough to handle, squeeze out excess liquid. Blend or process spinach with extra garlic, anchovy, juice and stock until pureed.

7 Serve veal and tomatoes with polenta and spinach mixture. If you like, top with extra oregano leaves.

TIPS

Polenta is the Italian answer to mashed potato – it's the perfect accompaniment for soaking up meat juices and too-good-to-waste sauces. It is available in regular and instant from supermarkets.

Braised chicken with
KUMARA & ONIONS

PREP + COOK TIME 1 HOUR SERVES 4

- 2 tablespoons olive oil
- 4 x 350g (11-ounce) chicken marylands
- 2 large red onions (600g), cut into wedges
- 2 medium kumara (orange sweet potato) (800g), sliced thickly
- 1 cup (250ml) gluten-free chicken stock
- 2 teaspoons 100% corn (maize) cornflour (cornstarch)
- 2 teaspoons water
- 4 sprigs fresh lemon thyme

1 Preheat oven to 180°C/350°F.

2 Heat oil in a 3-litre (12-cup) ovenproof dish over medium heat; cook chicken, skin-side down, for 5 minutes or until browned lightly, turn over. Arrange onion and kumara around chicken. Pour in stock, then blended cornflour and the water; bring to the boil. Add thyme, season.

3 Cover dish, transfer to oven; roast for 40 minutes or until chicken is cooked through and vegetables are tender. Serve topped with extra thyme sprigs, if you like.

TIPS

You can use chicken thigh cutlets or drumsticks in this recipe instead of chicken marylands.

Dairy free
NUT FREE
GLUTEN FREE
EGG FREE

**NUTRITIONAL
COUNT PER SERVING**
42.2g total fat
12g saturated fat
3039kJ (739 cal)
37.8g carbohydrate
49.2g protein
7.5g fibre

EGG FREE
GLUTEN FREE

**NUTRITIONAL
COUNT PER SERVING**
39.3g total fat
8.9g saturated fat
3231kJ (773 cal)
29.8g carbohydrate
70.9g protein
8.5g fibre

Baked salmon with
SPINACH & QUINOA SALAD

PREP + COOK TIME 40 MINUTES SERVES 4

- ½ cup (100g) quinoa
- 1 cup (250ml) water
- 4 x 220g (7-ounce) salmon fillets, skin on
- 2 tablespoons bottled basil pesto
- 1 clove garlic, crushed
- 250g (8 ounces) truss cherry tomatoes
- 2 trimmed cobs corn (500g)
- 120g (4 ounces) baby spinach leaves
- 1 tablespoon lemon juice
- 1 tablespoon extra virgin olive oil
- 1 clove garlic, extra, crushed

TIPS

Swap salmon for tuna or chicken breast fillets.

1 Preheat oven to 200°C/400°F.

2 Rinse quinoa under running cold water until water runs clear; drain well. Place quinoa in a medium saucepan with the water; bring to the boil. Reduce heat to low; cook, covered, for 15 minutes or until liquid is absorbed. Cool.

3 Meanwhile, rub salmon with combined pesto and garlic; place on a large baking dish with tomatoes. Bake for 15 minutes or until salmon is cooked as desired. Transfer salmon to a plate; cover, stand for 5 minutes.

4 Boil, steam or microwave corn until tender. When corn is cool enough to handle, cut kernels from cobs.

5 Place quinoa and kernels in a large bowl with spinach and combined juice, oil and extra garlic; toss gently to combine.

6 Serve salmon and tomatoes with quinoa salad, and with lemon wedges and baby basil leaves, if you like.

Honey-roasted hainanese
CHICKEN RICE BANQUET

PREP + COOK TIME 2 HOURS 20 MINUTES (+ REFRIGERATION) **SERVES** 6

You will need to start this recipe the day before.

- 1.6kg (3¼-pound) whole chicken
- 2 tablespoons rock salt
- 2 green onions (scallions), cut into 5cm (2-inch) lengths
- 50g (1½-ounce) piece ginger, sliced
- 2 tablespoons honey
- 2 teaspoons chinese five spice
- ¼ teaspoon ground white pepper
- 2 tablespoons rice wine vinegar
- 2 tablespoons gluten-free soy sauce
- 1 lebanese cucumber (130g)
- 1 tablespoon rice wine vinegar, extra
- 1 cup loosely packed coriander (cilantro) sprigs
- sliced fresh long red chilli and gluten-free soy sauce, to serve

BROTH

- 1 litre (4 cups) gluten-free chicken stock
- 1 litre (4 cups) water
- 300g (9½ ounces) daikon, chopped finely
- 2 green onions (scallions), cut into 5cm (2-inch) lengths
- 50g (1½-ounce) piece ginger, sliced

RICE

- 1 litre (4 cups) gluten-free chicken stock
- 15g (½-ounce) piece ginger, sliced
- 2 cloves garlic, unpeeled, bruised
- 2 cups (400g) medium-grain brown rice

CHILLI GINGER SAUCE

- 2 fresh long red chillies, chopped coarsely
- 3 large cloves garlic, chopped
- 50g (1½-ounce) piece ginger, peeled, chopped
- 1 green onion (scallion), chopped
- 2 tablespoons gluten-free soy sauce
- 1 teaspoon honey

1 Rub chicken all over with salt; rinse in cold water, pat dry with paper towel.

2 Fill chicken cavity with green onion and ginger; secure legs with kitchen string. Whisk honey, five spice, pepper, vinegar and sauce in a large bowl, add chicken; turn to coat. Leave, breast-side down, in marinade. Cover; refrigerate, overnight, turning occasionally.

3 Preheat oven to 240°C/475°F.

4 Meanwhile, place broth ingredients in a medium saucepan; season. Bring to the boil. Reduce heat; simmer for 30 minutes, skimming foam off during cooking.

5 Remove chicken from marinade, place in a roasting pan; discard marinade. Roast chicken for 20 minutes. Reduce oven to 200°C/400°F; roast a further 50 minutes or until juices run clear when the thickest part of a thigh is pierced. Cover; keep warm.

6 Meanwhile, make rice.

7 Process chilli ginger sauce ingredients until smooth.

8 Using a julienne peeler or spiraliser, cut cucumber into 'spaghetti'; combine with extra vinegar in a small bowl.

9 Cut chicken into six pieces. Place rice in serving bowls, top with chicken and cucumber 'spaghetti'. Spoon broth over rice and pan juices over chicken; top with coriander. Serve with chilli ginger sauce, sliced chilli and extra gluten-free soy.

rice Bring stock, ginger and garlic to the boil in a medium saucepan; stir in rice. Reduce heat to low; cook, covered, for 45 minutes or until liquid is absorbed.

Dairy free
NUT FREE
GLUTEN FREE
EGG FREE

**NUTRITIONAL
COUNT PER SERVING**
19.4g total fat
5.5g saturated fat
2537kJ (606 cal)
69g carbohydrate
36.6g protein
5g fibre

EGG FREE
GLUTEN FREE

**NUTRITIONAL
COUNT PER SERVING**
36g total fat
7.7g saturated fat
2039kJ (487 cal)
3.8g carbohydrate
36g protein
2.7g fibre

Pesto lamb with zucchini
& ALMOND SALAD

PREP + COOK TIME 25 MINUTES **SERVES** 4

- ⅓ cup (90g) pesto
- 4 lamb rump steaks (600g)

ZUCCHINI & ALMOND SALAD
- 3 medium zucchini (360g), cut into thin ribbons
- ⅓ cup (45g) blanched almonds, halved, roasted
- 1 small fresh red thai (serrano) chilli, chopped finely
- 1 tablespoon lemon juice
- 2 tablespoons extra virgin olive oil

1 Combine pesto and lamb in a large bowl. Cook lamb on a heated oiled grill plate (or grill or barbecue), for 4 minutes each side or until cooked as desired. Remove lamb from heat; cover with foil, rest for 5 minutes.
2 Make zucchini and almond salad.
3 Serve lamb with salad.

zucchini & almond salad Place ingredients in a large bowl; toss gently until zucchini is well coated in dressing. Season.

TIPS

Lamb can be marinated in pesto 2 hours ahead or overnight. You can also use lamb cutlets. Remove membranes and seeds from chilli to lessen the heat. Dress salad just before serving.

Basic gluten-free
FILLO-STYLE PASTRY

PREP TIME 1 HOUR **MAKES** 1KG (2 POUNDS)

- 3⅔ cups (495g) gluten-free plain (all purpose) flour
- 1½ cup (375ml) water
- 1 tablespoon xanthan gum
- 2 teapoons salt
- 125g (4 ounces) dairy-free spread

1 Blend or process flour, the water, gum, salt and dairy-free spread until mixture comes together. Turn onto a floured surface; knead lightly until smooth.

2 Divide dough into quarters. Wrap each quarter in plastic wrap.

3 Using one quarter of the pastry at a time; roll about a one-sixth of the dough on a surface lightly dusted with cornflour until thick enough to roll through the thickest setting on a pasta machine. Pass the dough through the pasta machine on each setting twice, dusting in a little cornflour when needed. Pass through to the third thinnest setting or until dough is about 1mm thick.

4 Following the recipes on pages 144 & 145 (see tips); cut dough as needed.

5 Repeat process with remaining dough.

tips You will need a quarter of the dough for each recipe on pages 144 & 145. The dough can be made a day ahead. Cover in plastic wrap and leave at room temperature. Dough can be used for tarts, toppings for pies as well as savoury pasties.

Dairy free
EGG FREE
GLUTEN FREE

NUTRITIONAL
COUNT PER 1KG
DOUGH
82.7g total fat
22g saturated fat
10580kJ (2531 cal)
425g carbohydrate
16.1g protein
0g fibre

4 ways with
FILLO-STYLE PASTRY

Dairy free
GLUTEN FREE

NUTRITIONAL COUNT PER PIE
27g total fat
8.8g saturated fat
2228kJ (533 cal)
29.6g carbohydrate
42.4g protein
1.1g fibre

GLUTEN FREE

NUTRITIONAL COUNT PER TRIANGLE
5.5g total fat
2.4g saturated fat
5147kJ (123 cal)
14.1g carbohydrate
4g protein
0.1g fibre

RICOTTA & SPINACH TRIANGLES

PREP + COOK TIME 1½ HOURS **MAKES 8**

Make basic gluten-free fillo-style pastry from page 142. Preheat oven to 220°C/425°F. Pour boiling water over 50g (3oz) baby spinach leaves to wilt; drain. When cool enough to handle, squeeze out excess water; chop coarsely. Combine spinach with 150g (4½oz) fresh ricotta and ¼ cup (25g) coarsely grated mozzarella; season. Using one quarter of the dough, roll dough according to recipe on page 142. Cut pastry into eight 10cm x 30cm (4-inch x 12-inch) strips. Place 3 teaspoons ricotta mixture at one end of each strip. Fold corner end of pastry diagonally over the filling to the other edge to form a triangle. Continue folding to the end of the strip to retain triangular shape. Repeat with remaining filling and pastry strips. Place on a baking-paper-lined tray; brush with combined 1 egg and 1 tablespoon milk. Bake for 20 minutes or until browned and crisp.

TIPS Triangles can be prepared a day ahead; store, covered, in the refrigerator. Bake just before serving.

PORK & FENNEL POT PIES

PREP + COOK TIME 1¾ HOURS **MAKES 4**

Make basic gluten-free fillo-style pastry on page 142. Preheat oven to 220°C/425°F. Heat 2 teaspoons olive oil in a medium frying pan over high heat; cook 2 cloves crushed garlic, 1 finely chopped small onion, 1 teaspoon each fennel seeds and ground coriander and ½ teaspoon sweet paprika, stirring, 5 minutes or until onion is soft and spices fragrant. Add 750g (1½lbs) pork mince; cook, stirring, until pork changes colour. Stir in 1 cup (250ml) gluten-free vegetable stock and 2 tablespoons tomato paste; simmer for 10 minutes or until thickened. Spoon mixture into four ¾-cup (180ml) ovenproof dishes. Using one quarter of the dough, roll dough according to recipe on page 142. Cut dough into eight 10cm (4-in) rounds. Place two rounds on each dish; brush top with combined 1 egg yolk and 1 tablespoon milk, sprinkle with 2 teaspoons fennel seeds. Place on a baking tray. Bake pies for 20 minutes or until pastry is golden brown.

NUTRITIONAL COUNT PER TART
11.5g total fat
5.1g saturated fat
690kJ (165 cal)
9.3g carbohydrate
6.1g protein
0g fibre

GLUTEN FREE

NUTRITIONAL COUNT PER PASTIZZI
4.1g total fat
1.3g saturated fat
322kJ (77 cal)
6.3g carbohydrate
3.6g protein
0.2g fibre

GLUTEN FREE

PROSCIUTTO, PERSIAN FETTA & BASIL TARTS

PREP + COOK TIME 1½ HOURS MAKES 12

Make basic gluten-free fillo-style pastry on page 142. Preheat oven to 220°C/425°F. Using one quarter of the dough, roll dough according to recipe on page 142. Cut into twenty-four 9cm (3¾-in) squares. Grease a 12-hole ⅓ cup (80ml) muffin pan. Line holes with two squares of pastry brushing wth a little melted butter between layers. Bake for 15 minutes or until crisp. Cool. Divide 60g (2oz) torn prosciutto and 100g (3oz) persian fetta between tart cases. Combine 6 eggs and ¼ cup (60ml) cream in a small bowl; pour into tart cases. Bake tarts for 15 minutes or until egg is just set. Stand for 10 minutes before serving. Scatter with baby basil leaves, if you like.

TIPS Tart cases can be made up to 2 days ahead; store in an airtight container. Tarts are best made just before serving.

LAMB & PINE NUT PASTIZZIS

PREP + COOK TIME 1½ HOURS MAKES 18

Make basic gluten-free fillo-style pastry on page 142. Preheat oven to 220°C/425°F. Heat 2 teapoons olive oil in a large frying pan over high heat; cook ½ small finely chopped brown onion, 1 clove crushed garlic and ½ teaspoon each finely grated fresh ginger, ground cumin and ground coriander for 5 minutes or until onion is softened. Add 250g (8oz) lamb mince; cook, stirring, for 5 minutes or until mince is cooked through. Add 1 tablespoon greek-style yoghurt; cook, stirring, for 2 minutes or until thickened. Stir in 2 teaspoons toasted pine nuts, 1 tablespoon chopped fresh flat-leaf parsley and 1 teaspoon finely grated lemon rind. Using one quarter of the dough, roll dough according to recipe on page 142. Cut dough into 18 x 10cm (4-in) rounds. Place a heaped teaspoon of mince mixture on each round; brush edges with combined 1 egg yolk and 1 tablespoon milk. Pinch and twist the edges together. Place on a baking-paper-lined tray; brush with a little more egg mixture. Bake 20 minutes or until crisp and golden.

TIPS Pastizzis can be prepared a day ahead; store, covered, in the refrigerator. Bake just before serving.

Sweet

Crêpes with lemon curd
& BLUEBERRIES

PREP + COOK TIME 45 MINUTES (+ COOLING) **SERVES** 4 (MAKES 12 CRÊPES)

- 1 cup (180g) white rice flour
- ½ teaspoons xanthan gum
- 1 egg
- 2 cups (500ml) milk, approximately (see tips)
- 50g (1½ ounces) butter
- 125g (4 ounces) fresh blueberries

LEMON CURD

- 3 egg yolks
- 2 teaspoons finely grated lemon rind
- ¼ cup (60ml) lemon juice
- ⅓ cup (75g) caster (superfine) sugar
- 80g (2½ ounces) butter

1 Make lemon curd.

2 Sift flour and gum in a medium bowl; make a well in the centre. Add combined egg and milk, gradually whisk until smooth. Pour batter into a large jug.

3 Melt a little of the butter in a 14cm (5½-inch) (base measurement) non-stick frying pan over medium heat. Pour 2 tablespoons of the batter into pan, tilting pan to coat base; cook over low heat for 1 minute or until browned lightly, loosening around the edge with a spatula. Turn crêpe; cook 1 minute or until browned. Remove crêpe from pan; cover to keep warm. Repeat with remaining butter and batter to make 12 crêpes in total.

4 Serve crêpes with curd and blueberries. Sprinkle with shredded lemon rind and dust with icing sugar, if you like.

lemon curd Combine ingredients in a small heatproof bowl over a small saucepan of simmering water, stirring constantly, for 15 minutes or until mixture thickens slightly and coats the back of a spoon. Remove from heat. Cover surface with plastic wrap; refrigerate until curd is cold.

TIPS

Depending on the weather, temperature, humidity or the batch of flour you have, you may need to use more or less milk. The mixture should be runny and not too thick; it should spread in the pan easily. Crêpes can be frozen for up to 3 months. Freeze crêpes layered between baking paper.

NUT FREE
GLUTEN FREE

NUTRITIONAL
COUNT PER SERVING
35g total fat
21.6g saturated fat
2592kJ (620 cal)
67.4g carbohydrate
10g protein
1.1g fibre

**NUTRITIONAL
COUNT PER CAKE**
13.8g total fat
1.1g saturated fat
813kJ (194 cal)
10g carbohydrate
6.3g protein
3g fibre

Peach & pistachio
CAKE POTS

PREP + COOK TIME 45 MINUTES **MAKES** 12

- 4 small peaches (460g), halved
- 1 cup (280g) greek-style yoghurt
- 2 medium apples (300g), grated coarsely
- 2 eggs, beaten lightly
- ¼ cup (60ml) milk
- 2 tablespoons honey
- 2 cups (240g) ground almonds
- 2 teaspoons baking powder
- ⅓ cup (45g) pistachios, chopped coarsely
- 1½ tablespoons honey, extra

1 Preheat oven to 180°C/350°F. Cut 12 x 12cm (4-inch) squares from baking paper; line 12 x ⅓ cup (80ml) ovenproof pots with paper squares (see tips).

2 Thinly slice three of the peaches. Coarsely chop remaining peach; blend or process to a coarse puree. Fold peach puree through yoghurt in a small bowl; cover and refrigerate until required.

3 Place apple, egg, milk, honey, ground almonds and baking powder in a large bowl; mix until just combined. Spoon mixture into pots; push peach slices 2cm (¾-inch) into the top of the batter.

4 Bake for 30 minutes or until a skewer inserted in the centre comes out clean.

5 Top cakes with pistachios; drizzle with extra honey. Serve warm or at room temperature with peach yoghurt.

TIPS

We used peat seedling pots available from hardware stores and garden nurseries. You can also cook the cakes in a 12-hole (⅓ cup/80ml) muffin pan, lined with baking paper squares. This recipe is best made on the day of serving.

Coconut & berry
CHIA PUDDING

PREP TIME 15 MINUTES (+ REFRIGERATION) SERVES 6

- 2½ cups (625ml) coconut milk
- ⅓ cup (55g) white chia seeds
- 1 teaspoon vanilla extract
- 2 tablespoons honey or pure maple syrup
- 1 medium banana (200g), chopped coarsely
- 1 tablespoon finely grated orange rind
- 3 cups (300g) mixed berries (see tips)
- micro mint or small mint leaves, to serve

1 Place coconut milk, seeds, extract and honey in a large bowl. Cover; refrigerate for 1 hour or overnight until thick.

2 Blend or process coconut milk mixture with banana, rind and 2 cups of the berries. Spoon into six ¾-cup (180ml) serving glasses; refrigerate for 30 minutes or until pudding has thickened.

3 Serve puddings topped with remaining berries and mint.

TIPS

Use whatever combination of berries you like, including cherries. If you have one, use a Thermomix or Vitamix to achieve a very smooth pudding consistency. Puddings can be made a day ahead; store, covered, in the fridge. Top with extra berries just before serving.

Dairy free
NUT FREE
GLUTEN FREE
EGG FREE

**NUTRITIONAL
COUNT PER SERVING**
24.6g total fat
19.2g saturated fat
1418kJ (338 cal)
21.9g carbohydrate
5g protein
4.6g fibre

chia

Dairy free
NUT FREE
GLUTEN FREE
EGG FREE

**NUTRITIONAL
COUNT PER SERVING**
23g total fat
7.4g saturated fat
2464kJ (588 cal)
93.4g carbohydrate
2.7g protein
4.3g fibre

Raspberry &
BANANA BREAD

PREP + COOK TIME 1¾ HOURS (+ COOLING) **SERVES 8**

You need 3 large (690g) overripe bananas for the mashed banana in this recipe.

- 1½ cups (350g) mashed banana
- ½ cup (125ml) vegetable oil
- ½ cup (125ml) soy milk
- 2½ cups (335g) gluten-free self-raising flour
- 1¼ cups (275g) firmly packed brown sugar
- ½ teaspoon bicarbonate of soda (baking soda)
- 1 cup (80g) desiccated coconut
- 1 cup (150g) frozen raspberries
- 20g (¾ ounce) dairy-free spread
- 1 large banana (230g), sliced thickly diagonally
- ⅓ cup (100g) golden syrup

1 Preheat oven to 180°C/375°F. Grease a 10cm x 20cm (4-inch x 8-inch) loaf pan; line base and long sides with baking paper, extending the paper 5cm (2 inches) over the sides.

2 Combine mashed banana, oil and milk in a small bowl.

3 Combine sifted flour, sugar and bicarbonate of soda with coconut in a large bowl. Make a well in the centre. Pour banana mixture into well; stir to combine. Fold in raspberries until just combined. Spoon mixture into pan; smooth the surface.

4 Bake bread for 1¼ hours or until a skewer inserted into the centre comes out clean. Stand bread in pan for 5 minutes before turning, top-side up, onto a wire rack to cool.

5 Melt dairy-free spread in a large frying pan over high heat, add sliced banana; cook 1 minute each side or until caramelised.

6 Serve thick slices of bread topped with banana and drizzled with golden syrup.

TIPS

Use your favourite dairy-free milk for this recipe. You can replace the raspberries with blueberries or chopped pear, or leave the fruit out altogether. Cut the bread into portion-sized slices and freeze in an airtight container for up to 3 months. The bread can be toasted to serve.

Passionfruit jelly with
POACHED PINEAPPLE

PREP + COOK TIME 35 MINUTES (+ REFRIGERATION) **SERVES** 6

- 12 passionfruit
- ¾ cup (180ml) fresh orange juice, strained
- ¼ cup (60ml) fresh lemon juice, strained
- ¾ cup (165g) caster (superfine) sugar
- 1 cup (250ml) water
- 1 tablespoon powdered gelatine
- ⅓ cup (80ml) boiling water
- ½ cup (40g) flaked coconut or shaved fresh coconut, toasted

POACHED PINEAPPLE

- 1 small pineapple (900g)
- 1 cup (220g) caster (superfine) sugar
- 1 cup (250ml) water
- 10cm (4-inch) stick fresh lemon grass (20g), halved lengthways
- 4 fresh kaffir lime leaves, crushed

1 Halve passionfruit; scoop pulp into a fine sieve over a 2-cup (500ml) measuring jug. Press to extract as much juice as possible. Discard seeds. Add orange and lemon juices to passionfruit juice; you should have 2 cups juice.

2 Place juice in a medium saucepan with sugar and the water; stir over high heat, without boiling, until sugar dissolves. Bring to the boil; remove from heat.

3 Sprinkle gelatine over the boiling water in a small heatproof jug. Stand jug in a small saucepan of simmering water; stir until gelatine dissolves. Stir gelatine mixture into juice mixture.

4 Pour jelly mixture into six 1-cup (250ml) glasses. Cover; refrigerate 4 hours or until set.

5 Meanwhile, make poached pineapple.

6 Serve jellies topped with poached pineapple and coconut.

poached pineapple Peel pineapple; cut in half lengthways. Slice each half into very thin slices. Place sugar and the water in a medium saucepan; stir over high heat, without boiling, until sugar dissolves. Add lemon grass to syrup with lime leaves; bring to the boil. Reduce heat; simmer, uncovered, for about 5 minutes. Add pineapple; simmer, uncovered, for 3 minutes or until pineapple is tender. Transfer pineapple mixture to a medium heatproof bowl. Cover; refrigerate 2 hours.

TIPS

To toast the coconut, stir in a medium frying pan over low-medium heat for 3 minutes or until golden. Remove coconut from pan immediately to prevent over-browning. Fresh coconut can be shaved using a vegetable peeler.

Dairy free
NUT FREE
GLUTEN FREE
EGG FREE

**NUTRITIONAL
COUNT PER SERVING**
4.6g total fat
3.8g saturated fat
1574kJ (376 cal)
76.9g carbohydrate;
4.6g protein
7.5g fibre

NUTRITIONAL COUNT PER PIECE
11.3g total fat
2.6g saturated fat
861kJ (206 cal)
23.3g carbohydrate
3.1g protein
0.3g fibre

Salted popcorn
& NUT SLICE

PREP + COOK TIME 15 MINUTES (+ COOLING) **MAKES** 20 PIECES

- 3 cups (45g) salted natural popped popcorn
- 1 cup (150g) roasted salted macadamias, chopped
- 1 cup (160g) roasted salted peanuts, chopped
- 1 cup (80g) roasted coconut chips
- 1½ cups (450g) honey

1 Line an oven tray with baking paper.

2 Combine popcorn, nuts and coconut in a medium bowl. Place honey in a frying pan over medium-high heat; bring to the boil. Reduce heat; simmer for 5 minutes or until honey starts to caramelise. (Make sure you watch the mixture, once it starts to caramelise it can quickly burn.)

3 Immediately pour honey over popcorn mixture; stir quickly to combine. Using a spatula, scrape mixture out onto the tray; cover with a piece of baking paper. Using a rolling pin, roll out flat; remove top layer of paper, leave to cool and set. Serve cut into pieces.

TIPS

You can use any kind of nuts in this recipe. This slice can be stored in an airtight container in the fridge for up to 2 weeks.

Dairy free
GLUTEN FREE

**NUTRITIONAL
COUNT PER SERVING**
33g total fat
3.9g saturated fat
2495kJ (596 cal)
71.7g carbohydrate
4.6g protein
2.6g fibre

Carrot cake with
TOFUTTI FROSTING

PREP + COOK TIME 1½ HOURS (+ COOLING) **SERVES** 12

- 2½ cups (335g) gluten-free self-raising flour
- ½ teaspoon bicarbonate of soda (baking soda)
- 2 teaspoons mixed spice
- ½ cup (35g) gluten-free baby rice cereal
- 1⅓ cups (295g) firmly packed brown sugar
- 3 cups (450g) coarsely grated carrot
- 1 cup (120g) coarsely chopped walnuts
- 3 eggs
- 1 cup (250ml) vegetable oil
- ½ cup (60g) coarsely chopped walnuts, extra

TOFUTTI FROSTING

- 100g (3 ounces) tofutti better than cream cheese, softened (see tips)
- 1 teaspoon finely grated lemon rind
- 1½ cups (240g) gluten-free icing sugar (confectioners' sugar)

1 Preheat oven to 180°C/350°F. Grease a deep 22cm (9-inch) round cake pan; line base and sides with baking paper.

2 Sift flour, soda and spice into a large bowl; stir in rice cereal, sugar, carrot and nuts. Stir in combined eggs and oil until smooth. Pour mixture into pan, smooth the surface.

3 Bake cake for 1¼ hours or until a skewer inserted comes out clean. Stand cake in pan 5 minutes; turn, top-side up, on a wire rack to cool.

4 Make tofutti frosting; spread on top of cooled cake. Top cake with extra walnuts.

tofutti frosting Beat tofutti and rind in a small bowl with an electric mixer until light and fluffy. Gradually beat in sifted icing sugar until smooth.

TIPS

'Tofutti better than cream cheese' is a tofu-based dairy-free cream cheese substitute, available in the refrigerated section of health food stores and major supermarkets. If you are not dairy intolerant, you can replace tofutti with cream cheese.

Strawberry
HALVA MOUSSE

PREP TIME 30 MINUTES (+ FREEZING & REFRIGERATION) **SERVES** 6

- 2 cups (500ml) coconut cream (see tips)
- 250g (8 ounces) strawberries
- ¼ cup (90g) honey
- 2 teaspoons vanilla extract
- 1 cup (280g) greek-style yoghurt
- ¾ cup (210g) unhulled tahini (sesame seed paste)
- 250g (8 ounces) strawberries, extra, sliced
- ⅓ cup (65g) pomegranate seeds
- ¼ cup (35g) pistachios, chopped
- 1 tablespoon sesame seeds, toasted

1 Pour coconut cream into a medium metal bowl; place in the freezer for 30 minutes or until chilled.

2 Blend or process strawberries, 1 tablespoon of the honey and half the extract until smooth.

3 Whisk chilled coconut cream with yoghurt, tahini and remaining honey and extract until thickened slightly, then swirl through the strawberry mixture.

4 Spoon mixture into six 1-cup (250ml) serving glasses. Cover; refrigerate for 2 hours or until firm.

5 Serve mousse topped with sliced strawberries, pomegranate seeds, pistachios and sesame seeds.

TIPS

Use a brand of coconut cream that states it is 100% natural on the label. Coconut cream that has 'emulsifying agents' added (it will state this on the label) may cause the mousse to separate into creamy and watery layers. You can make the mousse a day ahead; store, covered, in the fridge.

EGG FREE
GLUTEN FREE

**NUTRITIONAL
COUNT PER SERVING**
43g total fat
19.6g saturated fat
2482kJ (593 cal)
36.5g carbohydrate
15.7g protein
2.1g fibre

**NUTRITIONAL
COUNT PER SERVING**
26.3g total fat
3.1g saturated fat
1535kJ (366 cal)
19.7g carbohydrate
11.2g protein
5.7g fibre

Flourless almond, plum &
ORANGE BLOSSOM LOAF

PREP + COOK TIME 2¼ HOURS SERVES 6

- 2 medium green apples (300g), grated coarsely
- 2 eggs, beaten lightly
- ¼ cup (60ml) unsweetened almond milk
- 2 tablespoons honey or pure maple syrup
- 2 teaspoons vanilla extract
- 1 teaspoon orange blossom water
- 2 cups (240g) ground almonds
- 2 teaspoons gluten-free baking powder
- 5 small plums (375g), halved
- 2 teaspoons honey or pure maple syrup, extra
- 2 tablespoons flaked coconut, toasted

1 Preheat oven to 160°C/325°F. Grease a 10.5cm x 21cm x 6cm (4-inch x 8½-inch x 2½-inch) (base measurement) loaf pan; line base and long sides with baking paper extending the paper 5cm (2 inches) over the sides.

2 Combine apple, egg, almond milk, honey, extract and orange blossom water in a large bowl. Add ground almonds and baking powder; stir until just combined.

3 Spread mixture into pan, level surface; top with plums, cut-side up, pressing them slightly into the batter. Drizzle with extra honey.

4 Bake for 1¾ hours or until a skewer inserted into the centre comes out clean. Top with coconut and serve warm.

TIPS

You can also make this loaf with other stone fruit such as small peaches or apricots. You may need to cover the loaf loosely with baking paper during the last 10 minutes of baking to prevent overbrowning.

Apricot & pistachio
FROZEN YOGHURT

PREP + COOK TIME 1 HOUR (+ COOLING & FREEZING) **SERVES** 4

You need to start this recipe the day before serving.

- 1 cup (150g) dried apricots
- 2¼ cups (560ml) pure fresh apple juice
- 1 teaspoon ground cardamom
- 2¼ cups (630g) greek-style yoghurt
- ¼ cup (90g) honey
- 2 tablespoons sesame seeds, toasted
- ½ cup (70g) pistachios, chopped coarsely

1 Place apricots and juice in a medium frying pan; bring to the boil. Reduce heat; simmer for 15 minutes or until apricots are tender and plump and the juice is syrupy. Cool.

2 Process cooled apricot mixture with cardamom until smooth. Transfer mixture to a large bowl. Cover; refrigerate until required.

3 Combine yoghurt, honey, sesame seeds and half the pistachios in a medium bowl. Place yoghurt mixture in an ice-cream machine (see tips). Following the manufacturer's directions, churn mixture on the frozen yoghurt setting for 40 minutes until frozen. Spoon frozen yoghurt into the bowl with apricot mixture; fold the two mixtures together gently to create a marbled effect. Spoon into a 1.25-litre (5-cup) loaf pan, cover; freeze for 5 hours or overnight.

4 Serve frozen yoghurt topped with remaining pistachios.

TIPS

If you don't have an ice-cream machine, place yoghurt mixture only in the loaf pan, then cover with foil; freeze for 1 hour or until half frozen. Pulse the partially frozen mixture in a food processor to break-up ice crystals. Return to pan, cover with foil; repeat freezing and processing. Fold through apricot mixture, return to pan and cover with foil; freeze for 5 hours or overnight until frozen. Store yoghurt in the freezer for up to 2 weeks.

EGG FREE
GLUTEN FREE

**NUTRITIONAL
COUNT PER SERVING**
21.6g total fat
7.5g saturated fat
2550kJ (609 cal)
88.4g carbohydrate
15.8g protein
8.2g fibre

Dairy free
NUT FREE
GLUTEN FREE
EGG FREE

**NUTRITIONAL
COUNT PER SERVING**
0.3g total fat
0g saturated fat
134kJ (32 cal)
6.3g carbohydrate
0.5g protein
0.7g fibre

Watermelon & lemon
TEA GRANITA

PREP TIME 20 MINUTES (+ FREEZING) **SERVES** 6

You need to make this recipe the day before serving.

- 1 lemon herbal tea bag
- 1 cup (250ml) boiling water
- 1 tablespoon stevia granules or norbu (monk fruit sugar)
- 500g (1 pound) seedless watermelon, chopped
- 1½ tablespoons lemon juice
- 600g (1¼ pounds) seedless watermelon, extra, sliced thinly

FENNEL SALT
- 1 tablespoon sea salt flakes
- 1 teaspoon fennel seeds
- 1 teaspoon finely grated lemon rind

1 Steep the tea bag in the boiling water for 10 minutes; discard tea bag. Stir stevia into tea until dissolved.

2 Blend or process chopped watermelon until smooth. Stir in tea and juice. Pour mixture into a 2.8-litre (11-cup) shallow dish.

3 Freeze granita for 1 hour. Using a fork, break up any ice crystals. Freeze for a further 6 hours, scraping with a fork every hour or until frozen.

4 Make fennel salt.

5 Divide extra sliced watermelon among serving glasses, top with granita; sprinkle with fennel salt.

fennel salt Using a pestle and mortar, crush ingredients together.

Orange & white
CHOCOLATE BLONDIE

PREP + COOK TIME 1 HOUR (+ COOLING) **MAKES** 16 PIECES

- 150g (4½ ounces) white chocolate, chopped coarsely
- 100g (3 ounces) butter
- ⅔ cup (150g) caster (superfine) sugar
- 2 eggs, beaten lightly
- 2 teaspoons finely grated orange rind
- ¾ cup (100g) gluten-free plain (all-purpose) flour
- ½ cup (75g) tapioca flour
- ⅓ cup (50g) brown rice flour
- ½ cup (60g) ground almonds
- ⅓ cup (45g) coarsely chopped pistachios
- ¼ cup (90g) honey

1 Preheat oven 180°C/350°F. Grease a deep 19cm (8-inch) square cake pan; line base and sides with baking paper.

2 Stir chocolate and butter in a medium saucepan over low heat for 5 minutes or until chocolate melts and mixture is smooth. Remove from heat. Cool for 5 minutes.

3 Stir sugar into chocolate mixture; mixture may appear split at this stage, however it will come together once dry ingredients are added. Add egg and rind; stir to combine. Stir in sifted flours and ground almonds until combined. Pour into pan; sprinkle with pistachios.

4 Bake blondie for 40 minutes or until a skewer inserted in the centre comes out clean. Drizzle hot blondie with honey; cool in pan before cutting into 16 squares.

TIPS

Blondie can be made 3 days ahead; store in an airtight container.

GLUTEN
FREE

**NUTRITIONAL
COUNT PER PIECE**
12.3g total fat
5.8g saturated fat
1024kJ (245 cal)
31.2g carbohydrate
3.1g protein
0.6g fibre

EGG FREE
GLUTEN FREE

NUTRITIONAL COUNT PER SERVING
5g total fat
2.5g saturated fat
858kJ (205 cal)
32.5g carbohydrate
4.1g protein
5.5g fibre

Roasted pears with
CINNAMON LABNE

PREP + COOK TIME 1 HOUR (+ REFRIGERATION) **SERVES** 4

You need to start this recipe the day before.

- 1 cup (280g) low-fat greek-style yoghurt
- 2 herbal lemon tea bags
- 2 cups (500ml) boiling water
- 4 strips lemon rind
- 2 teaspoons honey
- 4 small firm pears (720g), peeled, halved, cored
- ½ teaspoon ground cinnamon
- 1 tablespoon chopped roasted hazelnuts

1 To make labne, line a medium sieve with a piece of muslin (or a clean Chux cloth); place sieve over a large bowl. Spoon yoghurt into muslin, cover with plastic wrap. Refrigerate overnight to drain; discard any liquid.

2 Preheat oven to 200°C/400°F.

3 Combine tea bags, the boiling water, rind and half the honey in a small bowl. Stand for 5 minutes. Drain; discard tea bags.

4 Place pears in a medium baking dish; pour over tea mixture. Transfer to oven; roast for 45 minutes, turning every 15 minutes, or until pears are tender.

5 Combine labne, cinnamon and remaining honey in a small bowl.

6 Serve pears with labne; drizzle with any pear cooking liquid and sprinkle with hazelnuts.

TIPS

Use a melon baller to core the pears. You can use bought labne in this recipe if you are running short of time.

Rosemary, labne
& ORANGE TART

PREP + COOK TIME 1½ HOURS (+ REFRIGERATION & COOLING) **SERVES** 8

You need to start this recipe the day before.

- 800g (1½ pounds) greek-style yoghurt
- 3 eggs
- 2 tablespoons honey
- 1 teaspoon vanilla extract
- 2 teaspoons finely chopped fresh rosemary leaves
- 2 cups (500ml) clear pure apple juice
- 1 sprig fresh rosemary, extra
- 3 small oranges (540g), sliced thinly

AMARANTH PASTRY

- 1½ cups (225g) fine amaranth flour
- 2 tablespoons arrowroot starch
- pinch salt
- ⅓ cup (70g) virgin coconut oil
- ½ cup (125ml) ice-cold water

TIPS

If you like, make the whole tart a day ahead and store in the fridge. Top with the oranges just before serving.

1 To make labne, line a medium sieve with a piece of muslin (or a clean Chux cloth); place sieve over a large bowl. Spoon yoghurt into muslin, cover with plastic wrap; refrigerate overnight to drain.

2 Make amaranth pastry.

3 Grease an 11cm x 34cm (4½-inch x 14-inch) rectangular loose-based fluted tart pan. Roll pastry between sheets of baking paper until 3mm (⅛-inch) thick. Lift pastry into pan, press into base and sides; trim excess pastry. Prick base all over with a fork. Cover; refrigerate for 30 minutes.

4 Preheat oven to 200°C/400°F.

5 Place tart pan on an oven tray; line pastry with baking paper, fill with dried beans or rice. Bake for 15 minutes. Remove paper and beans; bake a further 5 minutes or until browned lightly. Cool.

6 Reduce oven temperature to 140°C/285°F.

7 Drain labne; whisk in a large bowl with eggs, honey, extract and chopped rosemary. Spoon mixture into cooled pastry case. Bake for 25 minutes or until just set. Cool to room temperature. Refrigerate until cold.

8 Meanwhile, place apple juice and extra rosemary in a medium saucepan; bring to the boil over medium heat. Add orange slices to pan, reduce heat to low; simmer for 15 minutes or until tender. Cool.

9 Just before serving, drain orange slices and arrange over the cooled tart.

amaranth pastry Process flour, starch, salt and coconut oil until combined. With the motor operating, gradually add the iced water in a thin steady stream until a dough forms. Flatten pastry into a disc, wrap in plastic wrap; refrigerate for 30 minutes.

NUT FREE
GLUTEN FREE

**NUTRITIONAL
COUNT PER SERVING**
18.4g total fat
13g saturated fat
1719kJ (410 cal)
49.3g carbohydrate
11.4g protein
5.4g fibre

**NUTRITIONAL
COUNT PER PIECE**
15.6g total fat
10.2g saturated fat
1053kJ (251 cal)
24.5g carbohydrate
2.5g protein
2.5g fibre

Date & CASHEW SLICE

PREP + COOK TIME 20 MINUTES (+ STANDING & REFRIGERATION) **MAKES** 24 PIECES

- 1¾ cups (265g) raw cashews
- 1 cup (140g) coconut flour
- ¼ cup (60ml) melted coconut oil
- ¼ cup (60ml) maple syrup
- 1 tablespoon golden syrup
- 1½ cups (345g) fresh dates, pitted
- ¼ cup (60ml) melted coconut oil, extra
- ⅓ cup (115g) golden syrup, extra
- pinch salt
- 1 teaspoon vanilla essence

TOPPING

- ⅓ cup (35g) cacao powder
- ½ cup (125ml) melted coconut oil
- ¼ cup (60ml) maple syrup

1 Soak cashews in cold water for 1 hour; drain.

2 Grease a 16cm x 26cm (6½-inch x 10½-inch) rectangular slice pan; line base and long sides with baking paper, extending the paper 5cm (2 inches) over the sides.

3 Blend or process ¼ cup of the cashews, coconut flour, coconut oil and syrups until combined. Spread mixture into pan. Cover; refrigerate for 30 minutes or until set.

4 Meanwhile, blend or process remaining cashews with dates, extra oil, extra syrup, salt and essence until as smooth as possible. Spread date mixture over base. Cover; refrigerate for 30 minutes or until firmed slightly.

5 Make topping; pour over date filling, spread to cover evenly. Cover; refrigerate overnight.

6 Just before serving, cut into 24 squares.

topping Stir ingredients into a small bowl until smooth.

TIPS

The filling will work best if you use a Thermomix, Nutribullet, or other high-powered blender. We used Medjool fresh dates in this recipe. This slice can be stored in the fridge for up to 1 week.

Berry MOON ROCKS

PREP TIME 15 MINUTES (+ FREEZING) **SERVES** 4

- 250g (8 ounces) small strawberries, with stems on
- 175g (5½ ounces) blackberries
- 125g (4 ounces) raspberries
- 400g (12½ ounces) greek-style yoghurt
- 1½ tablespoons honey
- 1 vanilla bean, split lengthways, seeds scraped
- ⅔ cup (90g) finely chopped pistachios

1 Place all berries, separated in a single layer, on a tray; freeze for 30 minutes.

2 Combine yoghurt, honey, vanilla seeds and half the pistachios in a medium bowl. Add ½ cup of the frozen raspberries to the bowl, crush against the side of the bowl with a wooden spoon.

3 Using a toothpick, dip frozen berries, one at a time into the yoghurt mixture; place berries on a baking-paper-lined tray. Freeze for 3 hours until coating is set. Cover remaining yoghurt mixture; refrigerate.

4 Repeat dipping coated berries in remaining yoghurt mixture for a second coat; sprinkle with remaining pistachios. Freeze for 5 hours or overnight until frozen. Store in an airtight container in the freezer.

TIPS

Swap mango or pineapple chunks for berries. Use any leftover yoghurt for breakfast or on its own as a delicious snack. Store berry moon rocks in the freezer for up to 2 weeks.

**NUTRITIONAL
COUNT PER SERVING**
17.6g total fat
5.2g saturated fat
1449kJ (346 cal)
31.7g carbohydrate
11.9g protein
5.7g fibre

Dairy free
GLUTEN FREE

**NUTRITIONAL
COUNT PER PIECE**
7.5g total fat
2.6g saturated fat
798kJ (191 cal)
27.7g carbohydrate
1.7g protein
0.7g fibre

Almond, coconut
& PINEAPPLE SLICE

PREP + COOK TIME 1 HOUR 10 MINUTES **MAKES** 16 PIECES

- 125g (4 ounces) dairy-free spread
- 1 cup (220g) caster (superfine) sugar
- 1 egg, beaten lightly
- 1 cup (140g) coconut flour
- ½ cup (65g) gluten-free self-raising flour
- 2 tablespoons slivered almonds
- 440g (14 ounces) canned crushed pineapple, drained
- 225g (7 ounces) canned pineapple pieces, drained
- 300g (9½ ounces) pot-set plain yoghurt
- ¼ teaspoon ground cinnamon

TIPS

The pineapple needs to feel dry to touch. Pineapple can be swapped for pie apple or pears, if you like.

1 Preheat oven to 180°C/350°F. Grease a 20cm x 30cm (8-inch x 12-inch) rectangular slice pan; line base and sides with baking paper, extending the paper 5cm (2 inches) over the sides.

2 Beat dairy-free spread and sugar in a small bowl of an electric mixer until pale. Add egg, beat until just combined. Stir in combined sifted flours and almonds. Spread mixture into pan. Bake for 30 minutes or until browned and firm. Cool in pan.

3 Meanwhile, spread drained crushed pineapple and drained pineapple pieces onto two layers of paper towel. Stand 20 minutes. Coarsely chop pieces.

4 Spread crushed pineapple over cooled base, then top with chopped pieces; spread yoghurt over pineapple. Sprinkle with cinnamon.

5 Bake slice for another 20 minutes or until yoghurt is set. Cool in pan. Cut into 16 squares. Serve topped with toasted slivered almonds, if you like.

Raspberry &
CHOCOLATE BROWNIE

PREP + COOK TIME 50 MINUTES (+ COOLING) **MAKES** 24 PIECES

- 150g (4½ ounces) dairy-free spread
- 150g (4½ ounces) dairy-free dark chocolate
- 1 cup (250ml) almond milk
- 1¼ cups (275g) caster (superfine) sugar
- 3 eggs, beaten lightly
- ½ cup (65g) gluten-free plain (all-purpose) flour
- ½ cup (75g) buckwheat flour
- ¼ cup (35g) cacao powder
- 125g (4 ounces) fresh or frozen raspberries

1 Preheat oven to 180°C/350°F. Grease a 20cm x 30cm (8-inch x 12-inch) rectangular slice pan; line base and long sides with baking paper, extending the paper 5cm (2 inches) over the sides.

2 Combine spread, chocolate and almond milk in a medium saucepan over low heat; cook, stirring, for 5 minutes or until spread and chocolate are melted and mixture is smooth. Remove from heat; stir in sugar. Cool 10 minutes.

3 Beat eggs into chocolate mixture with a wooden spoon. Stir in combined, sifted flours and cacao. Gently fold through half the raspberries. Pour mixture into pan. Sprinkle with remaining raspberries.

4 Bake for 40 minutes or until a skewer inserted into the centre comes out clean. Cool in pan. Cut into 24 pieces. If you like, serve topped with fresh raspberries and dusted with a little extra cacao.

TIPS

Brownie can be made a day ahead.
Store in an airtight container.

Dairy free
GLUTEN FREE

**NUTRITIONAL
COUNT PER PIECE**
8.2g total fat
2.8g saturated fat
681kJ (163 cal)
20.9g carbohydrate
1.7g protein
0.9g fibre

NUT FREE
GLUTEN FREE

**NUTRITIONAL
COUNT PER COOKIE**
5.3g total fat
3.4g saturated fat
439kJ (105 cal)
13.9g carbohydrate
0.7g protein
0g fibre

Basic COOKIE DOUGH

PREP + COOK TIME 25 MINUTES (+ REFRIGERATION & COOLING) MAKES 20

- 125g (4 ounces) butter, softened
- ½ cup (110g) firmly packed brown sugar
- 1 teaspoon vanilla extract
- 1 egg
- 1¼ cups (170g) gluten-free plain (all-purpose) flour
- 2 tablespoons white rice flour
- ½ teaspoon bicarbonate of soda (baking soda)
- 1 teaspoon xanthan gum

1 Preheat oven to 180°C/350°F. Grease two oven trays; line with baking paper.

2 Beat butter, sugar and extract in a medium bowl with an electric mixer until just combined. Add egg; beat until just combined. Stir in sifted flours, soda and gum, in two batches. Cover; refrigerate 1 hour.

3 Using wet hands, roll tablespoons of mixture into balls; place 5cm (2 inches) apart on trays, flatten slightly.

4 Bake cookies for 18 minutes or until golden. Cool on trays.

TIPS

Cookies can be stored in an airtight container for up to 1 week.

4 ways with
COOKIE DOUGH

**NUTRITIONAL
COUNT PER COOKIE**
6g total fat
4g saturated fat
570kJ (136 cal)
20.1g carbohydrate
0.8g protein
0.3g fibre

**NUTRITIONAL
COUNT PER COOKIE**
7.4g total fat
4.6g saturated fat
581kJ (139 cal)
16.9g carbohydrate
1.2g protein
0.2g fibre

LEMON & COCONUT
COOKIES

PREP + COOK TIME 35 MINUTES
(+ REFRIGERATION & COOLING) **MAKES** 22

Following the basic cookie dough on page 185, omit vanilla
extract and replace with 2 teaspoons finely grated lemon rind.
Stir ½ cup (40g) desiccated coconut into the dough. Cover;
refrigerate 1 hour. Roll and bake dough according to recipe. Cool
on tray. Sift ¾ cup (165g) gluten-free icing sugar (confectioners'
sugar) into a small bowl; stir in 1 tablespoon lemon juice until
smooth, adding more if required to achieve desired consistency.
Drizzle icing over cookies; place on a wire rack to set.

TRIPLE CHOC
COOKIES

PREP + COOK TIME 30 MINUTES
(+ REFRIGERATION & COOLING) **MAKES** 24

Following the basic cookie dough on page 185, omit rice flour and
replace with 2 tablespoons cocoa powder. Stir ¼ cup (45g) each
of white choc bits, milk choc bits and dark choc bits into the
dough. Cover; refrigerate 1 hour. Roll and bake dough according
to recipe. Cool on tray.

NUTRITIONAL COUNT PER COOKIE
8.3g total fat
5.6g saturated fat
644kJ (154 cal)
18.9g carbohydrate
1.2g protein
0g fibre

NUTRITIONAL COUNT PER COOKIE
6.2g total fat
3.9g saturated fat
637kJ (152 cal)
23.5g carbohydrate
1g protein
0.2g fibre

CHOC CHIP COOKIES

PREP + COOK TIME 35 MINUTE
(+ REFRIGERATION & COOLING) **MAKES** 24

Following the basic cookie dough on page 185, stir ¾ cup (140g) dark choc bits into the dough. Cover; refrigerate 1 hour. Roll and bake dough according to recipe. Cool on tray. Stir 1 cup (150g) milk chocolate Melts and 2 teaspoons vegetable oil in a small heatproof bowl over a small saucepan of simmering water (don't let water touch base of bowl) until smooth. Dip cookies in melted chocolate until covered half way up. Place on tray to set.

WHITE CHOCOLATE & ORANGE COOKIES

PREP + COOK TIME 35 MINUTES
(+ REFRIGERATION & COOLING) **MAKES** 22

Following the basic cookie dough on page 185, omit vanilla extract and replace with 2 teaspoons finely grated orange rind. Stir ½ cup (95g) white choc bits and ¼ cup (40g) dried currants into the dough. Cover; refrigerate 1 hour. Roll and bake dough according to recipe. Cool on tray. Sift 1 cup (160g) gluten-free icing sugar (confectioners' sugar) into a bowl; stir in 1 tablespoon orange juice until smooth, adding more if required for desired consistency. Dip top of cookies in icing. Place on a wire rack to set.

Special
OCCASION

White chocolate &
PASSIONFRUIT ÉCLAIRS

PREP + COOK TIME 1 HOUR 20 MINUTES (+ COOLING) MAKES 12

- 80g (3 ounces) butter
- ⅔ cup (160ml) water
- 1 cup (135g) gluten-free plain (all-purpose) flour
- 1 teaspoon cream of tartar
- 4 eggs, beaten lightly
- 200g (6½ ounces) white chocolate, chopped coarsely

WHITE CHOCOLATE & PASSIONFRUIT FILLING

- 200g (6½ ounces) white chocolate, chopped coarsely
- ¾ cup (180ml) pouring cream
- 1 tablespoon passionfruit pulp

TIPS

Unfilled éclairs can be made 2 days ahead. Store in an airtight container. Pipe filling into éclairs just before serving.

1 Preheat oven to 200°C/400°F. Grease and line two baking trays with baking paper.

2 Place butter and the water in a medium saucepan over low heat until butter is melted. Bring to the boil. Add sifted flour and cream of tartar; cook, stirring, for 2 minutes or until mixture thickens and forms a ball. Remove from heat.

3 Transfer mixture to a medium bowl of an electric mixer. Beat in eggs, one at a time; beating until well combined between additions.

4 Spoon mixture into a large piping bag fitted with a plain 2cm (¾-inch) round tube. Pipe 12 x 10cm (4-inch) lengths, about 5cm (2 inches) apart, onto oven trays.

5 Bake éclairs for 30 minutes or until puffed and golden brown. Split éclairs lengthways; remove any soft dough from the centre. Return shells to trays; bake for a further 5 minutes to dry out the shells. Cool.

6 Meanwhile, make white chocolate and passionfruit filling.

7 Stir white chocolate in a small heatproof bowl over a small saucepan of simmering water (do not let the water touch the base of the bowl) until melted. Remove from pan. Dip top half of éclair shells onto melted white chocolate.

8 Fill a small disposable piping bag with the filling; cut a 1cm (½-inch) hole from end. Pipe filling into éclair bases; top with iced halves. Just before serving, drizzle with extra passionfruit, if you like.

white chocolate & passionfruit filling Place chocolate and cream in a small microwave safe bowl; microwave on MEDIUM (50%), in 30-second bursts, stirring, until melted and smooth. Refrigerate for 1 hour or until cold. Beat cold mixture in electric mixer on high until soft peaks form.

**NUTRITIONAL
COUNT PER ECLAIR**
23.2g total fat
14.5g saturated fat
1404kJ (336 cal)
28.3g carbohydrate
4.9g protein
0.2g fibre

Dairy free
EGG FREE
GLUTEN FREE

**NUTRITIONAL
COUNT PER SERVING**
62.2g total fat
12.4g saturated fat
3080kJ (736 cal)
36g carbohydrate
8.4g protein
7.7g fibre

Vegan brownie & strawberry
FROZEN CHEESECAKE

PREP TIME 20 MINUTES (+ FREEZING) **SERVES** 10

You will need to start this recipe the day before.

- 1½ cups (180g) pecans
- ⅓ cup (35g) dutch-processed cocoa
- 250g (8 ounces) fresh dates, pitted
- 1 teaspoon vanilla extract
- 4 cups (560g) raw macadamia halves
- 500g (1 pound) strawberries, chopped coarsely
- ½ cup (175g) rice malt syrup
- ¼ cup (60g) coconut oil
- 1 tablespoon vanilla extract, extra
- 2 tablespoons water
- 250g (8 ounces) strawberries, extra, halved
- 2 tablespoons rice malt syrup, extra

1 Grease and line base and side of a 20cm (8-inch) springform pan with baking paper.

2 Process pecans and cocoa until roughly chopped. With the motor operating, gradually add dates and extract, processing until mixture resembles coarse crumbs and holds together when pressed. Press mixture onto base of pan using the back of a spoon. Freeze for 30 minutes. Clean food processor bowl.

3 Process macadamias until roughly chopped. Add strawberries, syrup, solid coconut oil, extra extract and the water. Process for 2 minutes or until mixture is as smooth as possible. Pour mixture over brownie base. Freeze cheesecake for 4 hours or until very firm.

4 Using your hands, squeeze juice from 3 of the extra strawberries into a small bowl (discard pulp), add remaining extra strawberries and extra syrup; stir to combine. Just before serving, top cheesecake with strawberry mixture.

Champagne & orange
FRENCH MACAROON TRIFLE

PREP + COOK TIME 1 HOUR (+ REFRIGERATION) **SERVES** 10

- 7 gluten-free vanilla french macaroons (112g)
- 7 gluten-free blood orange french macaroons (112g)
- 2 tablespoons natural sliced almonds, toasted lightly

CHAMPAGNE & ORANGE JELLY
- 6 teaspoons gelatine
- 2 cups (500ml) fresh orange juice, strained
- 1 cup (250ml) champagne or sparkling wine
- ½ cup (110g) caster (superfine) sugar
- 2 medium oranges (480g)

CANDIED ORANGE RIND
- 2 medium oranges (480g)
- 1 cup (250ml) water
- ½ cup (110g) caster (superfine) sugar

ORANGE-SCENTED CUSTARD
- 1½ cups (375ml) thick gluten-free custard
- 1½ cups (375g) mascarpone cheese
- 2 tablespoons finely grated orange rind
- 1 tablespoon orange-flavoured liqueur

VANILLA CREAM
- 1 vanilla bean, split lengthways
- 2 cups (500ml) thickened (heavy) cream
- ¼ cup (40g) gluten-free icing sugar (confectioners' sugar)

1 Make champagne and orange jelly. Pour into a 3-litre (12-cup) deep glass dish. Cover; refrigerate 3 hours or until set.

2 Make candied orange rind, orange-scented custard and vanilla cream.

3 Just before serving, top jelly with macaroons, custard and cream. Top with almonds, candied rind and any syrup from the rind.

champagne & orange jelly Stir gelatine into ½ cup of the juice in a small bowl until combined. Stand 5 minutes. Place remaining juice, champagne and sugar in a medium saucepan over medium heat; stir until sugar is dissolved. Bring to the boil; boil about 1 minute. Remove from heat; stir in gelatine mixture until gelatine is dissolved. Segment oranges; add segments to juice mixture.

candied orange rind Remove rind from oranges with a zester. Place the water in a small saucepan; bring to the boil. Add rind; simmer about 1 minute. Drain rind; reserve ½ cup of the liquid. Place reserved liquid and sugar in same pan over medium heat; stir until sugar is dissolved. Bring to the boil; simmer, uncovered, about 1 minute. Add rind; simmer, uncovered, for 5 minutes or until candied. Drain. Spread out on a sheet of baking paper to cool.

orange-scented custard Whisk ingredients together in a large bowl.

vanilla cream Scrape seeds from vanilla bean. Beat cream, seeds and sugar in a medium bowl with an electric mixer until soft peaks form.

TIPS

Macaroons are available at bakeries or specialty food shops; if you can't find blood orange macaroons choose a plain orange or lemon flavour instead. You will need about 9 oranges for this recipe. Grate the rind from the oranges for the custard before juicing them for the jelly.

GLUTEN FREE

**NUTRITIONAL
COUNT PER SERVING**
48.3g total fat
31.2g saturated fat
2872kJ (686 cal)
54.7g carbohydrate
6.8g protein
3.7g fibre

GLUTEN FREE

NUTRITIONAL COUNT PER SERVING
36.9g total fat
23.7g saturated fat
2477kJ (592 cal)
64.2g carbohydrate
3.8g protein
1.8g fibre

Earl grey meringue
WITH SYRUP-SOAKED FIGS

PREP + COOK TIME 1 HOUR (+ COOLING) **SERVES** 8

- 2 earl grey tea bags
- 1 cup (220g) caster (superfine) sugar
- 4 egg whites, at room temperature
- 3 teaspoons 100% corn (maize) cornflour (cornstarch)
- 1 teaspoon white vinegar
- 2 tablespoons pistachios, chopped

SYRUP-SOAKED FIGS

- 2 earl grey tea bags
- 4 long strips orange rind
- 1 cup (220g) caster (superfine) sugar
- ½ cup (125ml) water
- ¼ cup (60ml) fresh orange juice
- 8 medium figs (480g), torn in half

SWEETENED MASCARPONE

- 500g (1 pound) mascarpone
- 1 teaspoon vanilla extract
- 1 tablespoon gluten-free icing sugar (confectioners' sugar)

1 Preheat oven to 150°C/300°F. Grease a large oven tray. Mark an 18cm x 30cm (7¼-inch x 12-inch) rectangle on a piece of baking paper; turn paper, marked-side down, onto tray.

2 Remove tea from bags; process with sugar until finely ground.

3 Beat egg whites in a medium bowl with an electric mixer until soft peaks form. Gradually add tea sugar mixture; beat until stiff and glossy. Sift cornflour over egg white mixture, add vinegar; fold in using a metal spoon. Spread mixture just inside marked rectangle on tray.

4 Reduce oven to 120°C/250°F; bake meringue 45 minutes or until firm to the touch. Turn oven off; cool in oven with door ajar, for at least 4 hours or overnight. (The top will crack a little but don't worry it will be covered with cream.)

5 Before serving, make syrup-soaked figs, then sweetened mascarpone.

6 Just before serving, spread sweetened mascarpone on meringue. Top with figs; spoon syrup over figs. Sprinkle with pistachios.

syrup-soaked figs Stir tea bags, rind, sugar, the water and juice in a medium saucepan over medium heat until sugar dissolves. Bring to the boil; cook for 6 minutes or until syrup thickens slightly. Place figs in a large bowl. Strain syrup over figs, gently stir to combine. Cool.

sweetened mascarpone Beat ingredients in a medium bowl with electric mixer until soft peaks form.

TIPS

Room temperature egg whites will beat better than cold ones. It is also a good idea when separating eggs, to do one egg at a time over a small bowl, adding to the mixer one by one; that way if you break a yolk you won't spoil the whole batch. The meringue can be made a day ahead; store in an airtight container at room temperature. Assemble just before serving.

Red velvet MUD CAKE

PREP + COOK TIME 1 HOUR 20 MINUTES (+ COOLING) **SERVES** 12

- 500g (1 pound) butter
- 300g (9½ ounces) white chocolate
- 4 cups (880g) caster (superfine) sugar
- 2 teaspoons vanilla essence
- 2 cups (500ml) milk
- 2 cups (270g) gluten-free plain (all-purpose) flour
- 1½ cups (200g) gluten-free self-raising flour
- ½ cup (90g) buckwheat flour
- 1 cup (80g) gluten-free baby rice cereal
- 2 tablespoons cocoa powder
- 6 eggs
- ¼ cup (60ml) liquid red food colouring

CREAM CHEESE FROSTING

- 80g (2½ ounces) butter, softened
- 190g (6 ounces) cream cheese, softened
- ¼ teaspoon vanilla essence
- 4 cups (640g) gluten-free icing sugar
  (confectioners' sugar)

1 Preheat oven to 180°C/350°F. Grease three deep 23cm (9-inch) round cake pans, line base and sides with baking paper.

2 Stir butter, chocolate, sugar, essence and milk in a large saucepan, over low heat until butter and chocolate are melted and mixture is smooth. Cool 10 minutes.

3 Combine sifted flours, rice cereal and cocoa powder in a large bowl, gradually whisk in combined eggs and cooled chocolate mixture with food colouring. Divide mixture evenly into pans.

4 Bake cakes for 1 hour or until a skewer inserted into the centre comes out clean. Cool cakes in pans.

5 Meanwhile, make cream cheese frosting.

6 Place one cake on a serving plate or stand, spread with 1 cup of the frosting. Layer with second cake and another cup of frosting. Finish with third cake and remaining frosting. Decorate with fresh or frozen reaspberries and white chocolate shavings, if you like.

cream cheese frosting Beat butter, cream cheese and essence in a small bowl of an electric mixer for 2 minutes until smooth. Add icing sugar, 1 cup at a time, beating well between additions. Scrape down sides of bowl and beat for a further 1 minute or until light and fluffy.

TIPS

The cake can be made 2 days ahead;
store, covered, in the fridge.

GLUTEN
FREE

NUTRITIONAL
COUNT PER SERVING
55.4g total fat
35.4g saturated fat
5260kJ (1257 cal)
188g carbohydrate
9g protein
0.5g fibre

GLUTEN FREE

**NUTRITIONAL
COUNT PER SERVING**
46.5g total fat
25.7g saturated fat
2702kJ (645 cal)
52.8g carbohydrate
6.9g protein
1.3g fibre

Lemon curd
MERINGUE CAKE

PREP + COOK TIME 1¾ HOURS (+ REFRIGERATION, COOLING & STANDING) **SERVES** 12

- 1 cup (150g) almonds
- 4 egg whites
- 1 cup (220g) caster (superfine) sugar
- 125g (4 ounces) white chocolate, grated coarsely
- 600ml thick (double) cream
- 125g (4 ounces) fresh blueberries

LEMON CURD
- 250g (8 ounces) cold butter, chopped coarsely
- 2 eggs, beaten lightly
- 2 egg yolks
- ⅔ cup (160ml) lemon juice
- 1⅓ cups (300g) caster (superfine) sugar

TIPS

Lemon curd can be made 2 days ahead; store, covered, in the fridge.

1 Make lemon curd.

2 Preheat oven to 160°C/325°F. Insert the base of a 24cm (9½-inch) springform pan upside down to make it easier to remove the cake. Grease and line base with baking paper.

3 Spread almonds, in a single layer, on an oven tray; roast, uncovered, for 12 minutes or until skins begin to split. Cool. Chop almonds finely.

4 Beat egg whites and ¼ cup of the sugar in a small bowl with an electric mixer until firm peaks form. Add remaining sugar; beat on high speed for 5 minutes or until sugar is dissolved. Fold in chocolate and almonds. Spread mixture into pan.

5 Bake meringue for about 40 minutes. Cool in pan.

6 Whisk cream in a small bowl with a wire whisk until soft peaks form; fold half the cream into lemon curd. Using a spoon, gently push down on meringue. Spoon curd mixture onto meringue. Refrigerate for 1 hour until firm.

7 Just before serving, top with remaining whipped cream and the blueberries.

lemon curd Place butter in a medium saucepan; strain beaten egg into pan. Add remaining ingredients; stir over low heat, without boiling, for 10 minutes or until mixture thickly coats the back of a spoon. Transfer curd to a medium heatproof bowl; cover surface directly with plastic wrap. Refrigerate until cold.

Macaroon, mango & lime
FROZEN YOGHURT CAKE

PREP + COOK TIME 1 HOUR (+ COOLING & FREEZING) SERVES 12

- 2 egg whites
- ½ cup (110g) caster (superfine) sugar
- 1 teaspoon vanilla bean paste
- 2 tablespoons gluten-free plain (all-purpose) flour
- 1½ cups (120g) desiccated coconut
- 1½ cups (420g) greek-style yoghurt
- 300ml thickened (heavy) cream
- 2 tablespoons gluten-free icing sugar (confectioners' sugar)
- 2 medium mangoes (860g), chopped
- 1 tablespoon finely grated lime rind
- 2 tablespoons lime juice
- 1 medium mango (430g), extra, sliced thinly
- 1 lime, sliced thinly

TIPS

If you don't have a loaf pan with the exact measurements, trim the macaroon layers to fit your pan. Cake can be made a 1 week ahead and frozen.

1 Preheat oven to 160°C/325°F. Grease a 20cm x 30cm (8-inch x 12-inch) slice pan; line base and two long sides with baking paper, extending the paper 5cm (2 inches) over the sides.

2 Beat egg whites in a small bowl with an electric mixer until soft peaks form. Gradually add sugar, beating until dissolved after each addition. Stir in vanilla paste, sifted flour and coconut in two batches. Spread mixture into pan; level the surface.

3 Bake macaroon for 20 minutes or until firm to touch and lightly browned. Cool in pan.

4 Line base and sides of a deep 14cm x 23cm (5½-inch x 9¼-inch) loaf pan with baking paper.

5 Beat yoghurt and cream in a small bowl with electric mixer until soft peaks form. Fold in icing sugar, chopped mango, rind and juice. Carefully pour a little more than one-third of the yoghurt mixture (2¼ cups) into loaf pan. Cut a 12cm x 20cm (4¾-inch x 8-inch) piece from half the macaroon; reserve remaining macaroon. Place trimmed macaroon on yoghurt mixture. Cover; freeze for 1 hour or until firm. Refrigerate remaining yoghurt mixture.

6 Pour remaining yoghurt mixture into pan. Cut a 14cm x 20cm (5½-inch x 8-inch) piece from remaining macaroon; place on yoghurt layer. Reserve remaining macaroon. Cover; freeze for 4 hours or overnight.

7 Turn cake onto a platter; stand 10 minutes before serving. Served topped with extra mango, lime slices and crushed remaining macaroon.

**NUTRITIONAL
COUNT PER SERVING**
18.4g total fat
12.8g saturated fat
1173kJ (280 cal)
24.2g carbohydrate
4.1g protein
2.5g fibre

NUT FREE
GLUTEN FREE

NUTRITIONAL COUNT PER BUN
11.9g total fat
2.5g saturated fat
1372kJ (328 cal)
50.7g carbohydrate
4g protein
0.9g fibre

HOT CROSS BUNS

PREP + COOK TIME 1½ HOURS (+ STANDING) **MAKES** 16

- 3 cups (405g) gluten-free plain (all-purpose) flour
- ½ cup (75g) potato flour
- ½ cup (80g) brown rice flour
- ½ cup (75g) tapioca flour
- 3 teaspoons mixed spice
- 1 teaspoon cinnamon
- 3 teaspoons (10g) dried yeast
- 2 teaspoons xanthan gum
- ¼ cup (55g) caster (superfine) sugar
- 3 egg whites
- 1 egg
- ¾ cup (180ml) olive oil
- 2 cups (500ml) milk
- 1 cup (160g) sultanas

FLOUR PASTE FOR CROSSES

- ½ cup (65g) gluten-free plain (all-purpose) flour
- 2 teaspoons caster (superfine) sugar
- ⅓ cup (80ml) water, approximately

GLAZE

- 1 tablespoon caster (superfine) sugar
- 1 teaspoon gelatine
- 1 tablespoon water

1 Grease a deep 23cm (9¼-inch) square cake pan.

2 Combine sifted flours, spices, yeast, gum and sugar in a large bowl.

3 Place egg whites, egg, oil and half the milk in a large bowl of an electric mixer; beat on medium speed for 3½ minutes. Add remaining milk and the flour mixture, 1 cup at a time, beating until combined and smooth. Fold through sultanas.

4 Divide dough into 16 pieces. With wet hands shape dough into balls. Place balls into pan; cover, stand in a warm place for 45 minutes.

5 Meanwhile, preheat oven to 220°C/425°F.

6 Make flour paste for crosses; place in a piping bag fitted with a small plain tube. Pipe crosses on buns.

7 Bake buns for 1 hour or until golden and the buns sound hollow when tapped. Transfer buns, top-side up, onto a wire rack.

8 Make glaze; brush tops of hot buns with hot glaze. Serve buns warm.

flour paste for crosses Combine flour and sugar in a small bowl. Gradually blend in enough of the water to form a smooth paste.

glaze Stir ingredients in a small saucepan over medium heat, without boiling, until sugar and gelatine dissolve.

TIPS

Hot cross buns are best served warm on the day you make them. Buns can be reheated in the microwave on HIGH (100%) in 10-second bursts until heated through.

Raspberry swirled
CHEESECAKE

PREP + COOK TIME 1 HOUR (+ COOLING & REFRIGERATION) **SERVES** 12

- 155g (5-ounce) packet gluten-free ginger nut biscuits
- 50g (1½ ounces) butter, melted
- 60g (2 ounces) fresh raspberries
- 1 tablespoon gluten-free icing sugar (confectioners' sugar)
- 4 eggs
- ¾ cup (165g) caster (superfine) sugar
- 500g (1 pound) cream cheese, softened
- 1 teaspoon vanilla bean paste

TIPS

You could swap raspberries for blueberries, if you like. Cheesecake can be made 2 days ahead.

1 Process biscuits until fine; add butter, process until combined. Spoon mixture evenly over base of a greased 20cm (8-inch) springform pan; press down firmly with a straight-sided glass or bottle. Place pan on an oven tray; refrigerate until required.

2 Preheat oven to 160°C/325°F.

3 Blend or process raspberries and icing sugar until smooth. Push puree through a fine sieve over a small bowl to remove the seeds; discard seeds.

4 Beat eggs and sugar in a small bowl with an electric mixer until thick and creamy. Beat cream cheese and vanilla paste in a medium bowl with electric mixer until smooth. Add egg mixture to cream cheese mixture; beat until combined. Pour over base in pan.

5 Using a teaspoon, spoon dots of raspberry puree on top of filling mixture; using a skewer to swirl raspberry.

6 Bake cheesecake for 40 minutes or until still slightly wobbly in the centre. Turn off oven; cool in oven with the door ajar. Refrigerate for 3 hours or overnight.

7 Serve cheesecake topped with fresh raspberries, if you like.

GLUTEN FREE

**NUTRITIONAL
COUNT PER SERVING**
47.7g total fat
27.5g saturated fat
2771kJ (663 cal)
56.1g carbohydrate
5.1g protein
1.9g fibre

Hazelnut meringue torte with
BANANA & BUTTERSCOTCH

PREP + COOK TIME 1¾ HOURS (+ COOLING) SERVES 12

- 6 egg whites
- 1½ cups (330g) caster (superfine) sugar
- ¾ teaspoon cream of tartar
- ⅔ cup (70g) ground hazelnuts
- 3 large bananas (690g), sliced
- ⅓ cup (45g) hazeluts, toasted, chopped coarsely

MASCARPONE FILLING

- 300g (9½ ounces) mascarpone
- 300ml thickened (heavy) cream
- 1 tablespoon gluten-free icing sugar
  (confectioners' sugar)
- 1 tablespoon hazelnut-flavoured liqueur

BUTTERSCOTCH SAUCE

- 180g (6 ounces) butter, chopped
- 1 cup (220g) firmly packed light brown sugar
- ¾ cup (180ml) thickened (heavy) cream

1 Preheat oven to 160°C/350°F. Grease two large oven trays. Draw two 18cm (7¼-inch) circles onto two sheets of baking paper; place baking paper, marked-side down, on trays.

2 Beat egg whites, sugar and cream of tartar in a medium bowl with an electric mixer on high for 10 minutes or until mixture is thick and glossy. Gently fold in the ground hazelnuts. Using a spatula, evenly spread meringue onto trays using markings as a guide.

3 Bake meringues for 1¼ hours or until firm. Cool in oven.

4 Meanwhile, make mascarpone filling, then butterscotch sauce.

5 Just before serving, place one meringue on a serving plate; top with a quarter of the mascarpone filling, a quarter of the sliced bananas and 2 tablespoons of the butterscotch sauce. Repeat with remaining meringues, filling, banana and sauce. Sprinkle with chopped hazelnuts.

mascarpone filling Beat mascarpone, cream and sugar in a small bowl of electric mixer until smooth; stir in liqueur.

butterscotch sauce Stir ingredients in a medium saucepan until butter is melted. Bring to the boil; simmer, uncovered, for 3 minutes. Cover; refrigerate until cold.

TIPS

We used Frangelico for the hazelnut-flavoured liqueur in this recipe. Meringues can be made a day ahead; store in airtight containers. Mascarpone filling and butterscotch sauce can be made a day ahead; store separately, covered, in the fridge. Assemble torte just before serving.

Salted coconut &
PASSIONFRUIT SEMIFREDDO

PREP + COOK TIME 30 MINUTES (+ FREEZING) **SERVES** 10

- 2 cups (500ml) coconut cream (see tips)
- 6 eggs, separated
- ⅓ cup (115g) honey or pure maple syrup
- 2 teaspoons vanilla extract
- ½ cup (50g) coconut milk powder
- 1 teaspoon sea salt flakes
- ⅓ cup (80ml) fresh passionfruit pulp
- ½ cup (25g) unsweetened coconut flakes
- ¼ cup (60ml) fresh passionfruit pulp, extra
- 1 tablespoon micro mint or small mint leaves

1 Pour coconut cream into a medium metal bowl; place in the freezer for 30 minutes or until chilled.

2 Grease a 9cm (3¾-inch) deep, 11.5cm x 20cm (4¾-inch x 8-inch) loaf pan; line with baking paper, extending the paper 5cm (2 inches) over the sides.

3 Beat egg yolks, 2 tablespoons of the honey and extract in a small bowl with an electric mixer on high for 5 minutes or until thick and pale. Transfer to a large bowl.

4 Beat egg whites in a clean small bowl with electric mixer until soft peaks form. Gradually add the remaining honey; beat until thick and glossy.

5 Whisk chilled coconut cream, milk powder and salt in a medium bowl until slightly thickened. Gently fold egg whites and coconut cream mixture into egg yolk mixture.

6 Pour mixture into pan; freeze for 1 hour or until mixture has thickened slightly. Swirl through passionfruit pulp; freeze for at least another 3 hours or overnight.

7 Stand semifreddo at room temperature for 5 minutes before inverting onto a platter. Top with coconut flakes, extra passionfruit and mint to serve.

TIPS

Use a brand of coconut cream that states it is 100% natural on the label. Coconut cream that has 'emulsifying agents' added (it will state this on the label) may cause the semifreddo to separate into creamy and watery layers. You will need about 9 passionfruit to get the amount of pulp required. You could also peel the flesh of fresh coconut with a vegetable peeler, if you prefer, and substitute it for the coconut flakes.

Dairy free
GLUTEN FREE

**NUTRITIONAL
COUNT PER SERVING**
17.7g total fat
14.1g saturated fat
988kJ (236 cal)
13.5g carbohydrate
5.6g protein
2.5g fibre

GLUTEN FREE

NUTRITIONAL COUNT PER SERVING
47.8g total fat
23.9g saturated fat
3708kJ (887 cal)
100.5g carbohydrate
15.7g protein
2.3g fibre

Cardamom & lemon cake
WITH VANILLA LABNE
& LEMON SYRUP

PREP + COOK TIME 2 HOURS (+ REFRIGERATION & STANDING) **SERVES** 8

You will need to start the labne a day ahead.

- 9 egg whites
- 270g (8½ ounces) butter, melted
- 1½ cups (180g) ground almonds
- 2¼ cups (360g) gluten-free icing sugar (confectioners' sugar)
- ¾ cup (100g) gluten-free plain (all-purpose) flour
- 1 tablespoon finely grated lemon rind
- 3 teaspoons ground cardamom

LEMON SYRUP
- ¾ cup (180ml) lemon juice
- 1½ cups (330g) caster (superfine) sugar
- 2 lemons, zested

VANILLA LABNE
- 1 vanilla bean
- 1kg (2 pounds) greek-style yoghurt
- ½ teaspoon salt
- 2 tablespoons caster (superfine) sugar

TIPS

Cake can be made 2 days ahead, store in an airtight container.

1 Make vanilla labne.

2 Preheat oven 160°C/325°F. Grease a deep 20cm (8-inch) round cake pan; line base and sides with baking paper.

3 Whisk egg whites, butter, almonds, icing sugar, sifted flour, rind and cardamom in a large bowl until well combined. Pour mixture into pan.

4 Bake cake for 1 hour 40 minutes; cover with foil halfway through cooking to prevent overbrowning, or until a skewer inserted comes out clean. Stand cake in pan for 10 minutes before turning top-side up on a wire rack over an oven tray.

5 Meanwhile, make lemon syrup. Pour hot syrup over hot cake.

6 Serve cooled cake with vanilla labne and reserved syrup and zest.

lemon syrup Stir ingredients in a small saucepan over medium heat until sugar dissolves. Bring to the boil; boil for 5 minutes or until syrup thickens. Remove from heat. Reserve 2 tablespoons syrup and zest.

vanilla labne Split vanilla bean in half lengthways; scrape seeds into a medium bowl. Discard pod. Add remaining ingredients; stir until combined. Spoon yoghurt mixture into a sieve lined with two layers of muslin (or a clean Chux cloth). Tie cloth close to yoghurt. Refrigerate 12 hours or overnight, squeezing the yoghurt occasionally, until thick. Stir yoghurt until smooth.

Mini GINGERBREAD HOUSES

PREP + COOK TIME 2 HOURS (+ REFRIGERATION & STANDING) MAKES 8

- 125g (4 ounces) butter, softened
- ½ cup (175g) golden syrup (or treacle)
- ½ cup (110g) firmly packed dark brown sugar
- 2½ cups (335g) gluten-free plain (all-purpose) flour
- 1 tablespoon ground ginger
- 1 teaspoon ground cinnamon
- ¼ teaspoon ground cloves
- 1 tablespoon xanthan gum
- gluten-free icing sugar (confectioners' sugar), for dusting

ROYAL ICING

- 1½ cups (240g) gluten-free icing sugar (confectioners' sugar)
- 1 egg white
- 1 teaspoon lemon juice

1 Using the templates from page 236, trace and cut out the shapes using firm card board.

2 Beat butter, syrup and sugar in a medium bowl with an electric mixer until creamy and paler in colour. Add combined sifted flour, spices and gum; stir until mixture just comes together. Knead dough gently on a surface lightly dusted with gluten-free plain flour until smooth. Cover with plastic wrap; refrigerate 30 minutes or until firm.

3 Preheat oven to 180°C/350°F. Grease two oven trays; line with baking paper.

4 To make side walls: roll one-third of the dough on a surface dusted with gluten-free flour until 3mm (⅛-inch) thick. Using wall template, cut out 16 squares; place 3cm (1¼ inches) apart on trays.

5 Bake for 10 minutes or until lightly golden. Slide paper and walls from trays onto a wire rack to cool. Cool and reline trays (see tips).

6 To make front and back walls: repeat with rolling half the remaining dough. Using end wall template, cut out 16 walls; place on trays. Bake as per instructions in step 5.

7 To make roof: repeat rolling remaining dough. Using roof template, cut out 16 rectangles; place on trays. Bake as per instructions in step 5.

8 Make royal icing. Fill piping bag fitted with a fine piping nozzle (no. 2). Pipe icing onto shapes, attaching side walls with front and back walls to make a house (hold in place for a few minutes to stabilise, if necessary). Pipe along the top edge with a little icing; position roof (hold in position, if necessary). Repeat with remaining pieces to make a total of 10 houses. Stand for 30 minutes or until icing is set.

9 Using picture as a guide decorate houses with royal icing. Stand for 30 minutes or until set. Dust with icing sugar.

royal icing Sift icing sugar through a fine sieve into a bowl. Lightly beat egg white in a small bowl with electric mixer until mixture is just broken up – do not whip into peaks. Beat in the icing sugar, a tablespoon at a time, to reach the required consistency. When icing reaches right consistency, stir in juice. Cover surface directly with plastic wrap until ready to use.

TIPS

Cool oven trays between baking gingerbread shapes; reline with baking paper before the next batch. Don't overcook the shapes; they will feel soft when cooked, but will crisp on standing. Use melted white chocolate to decorate instead of royal icing to make recipe completely egg-free. Gingerbread houses will keep in an airtight container for up to 1 week.

**NUTRITIONAL
COUNT PER HOUSE**
14.2g total fat
5.7g saturated fat
2098kJ (502 cal)
91.5g carbohydrate
4.1g protein
0g fibre

Caramel & almond mud cake
WITH CHEESECAKE FROSTING

PREP + COOK TIME 3 HOURS (+ COOLING) **SERVES** 12

- 360g (11½ ounces) white chocolate, chopped
- 200g (6½ ounces) butter, chopped
- 1⅓ cups (295g) firmly packed dark brown sugar
- 4 eggs
- 1½ cups (200g) gluten-free plain (all-purpose) flour
- 1 cup (150g) tapioca flour
- ⅔ cup (100g) brown rice flour
- 1 cup (120g) ground almonds

CHEESECAKE FROSTING

- 250g (8 ounces) cream cheese, softened
- 125g (4 ounces) butter, softened
- 1½ cups (240g) gluten-free icing sugar mixture (confectioners' sugar)
- rose pink food colouring

1 Preheat oven to 170°C/335°F. Grease a deep 22cm (9-inch) round cake pan; line base and sides with three layers of baking paper.

2 Stir chocolate and butter in a medium saucepan over medium heat for 3 minutes or until melted and smooth. Remove from heat; stand 10 minutes.

3 Whisk in sugar and eggs. Stir in sifted flours and ground almonds. Pour mixture into pan.

4 Bake for 2 hours 45 minutes, or until a skewer inserted in the centre comes out clean. Cover with foil during cooking to prevent overbrowning. Cool cake in pan.

5 Make cheesecake frosting. Spoon half the frosting into a piping bag fitted with a small star piping nozzle.

6 Level top of cake if necessary; split cake into two layers. Place bottom cake layer on a plate; spread with remaining frosting. Top with remaining cake layer; pipe remaining frosting over top of cake.

cheesecake frosting Beat cream cheese and butter in a small bowl with an electric mixer until smooth; gradually add sifted sugar until combined. Stir in enough food colouring to make filling light pink.

TIPS

Cake can be made 2 days ahead; store, covered, in the fridge. Remove from fridge 30 minutes before serving.

Banana, coffee & pecan
BUNDT CAKE

PREP + COOK TIME 1¼ HOURS (+ COOLING) **SERVES 12**

- 185g (6 ounces) dairy-free spread
- 1¼ cups (275g) caster (superfine) sugar
- 3 eggs
- 1 tablespoon espresso coffee granules
- 2 teaspoons boiling water
- 1¼ cups mashed banana
- 2¼ cups (365g) gluten-free self-raising flour
- ½ teaspoon bicarbonate of soda (baking soda)
- 1 tablespoon xanthan gum
- ⅓ cup (80ml) rice milk
- ½ cup (60g) coarsely chopped pecans

COFFEE PECANS

- 1 tablespoon espresso coffee granules
- ½ cup (125ml) water
- 1 cup (220g) caster (superfine) sugar
- 1 cup (120g) pecans

1 Preheat oven to 180°C/350°F. Grease a 21cm (8½-inch) bundt pan with dairy-free spread.

2 Beat spread and sugar in a small bowl with an electric mixer until light and fluffy. Add eggs, one at a time, beat until combined. Mix will split at this stage but will come back together once flour is added.

3 Transfer mixture to large bowl, stir in combined coffee and the water and banana; stir until well combined. Stir in the sifted flour, soda, gum, milk and chopped pecans, in two batches. Pour mixture into pan; smooth top.

4 Bake for 55 minutes or until a skewer inserted comes out clean. Turn cake onto a wire rack over a baking tray.

5 Meanwhile, make coffeed pecans. Top cake with coffee pecans and drizzle with hot reserved syrup.

coffee pecans Stir coffee, the water and sugar in a small saucepan over medium heat, about 5 minutes or until sugar dissolves. Bring to the boil; reduce heat, simmer 5 minutes or until thickened. Remove from heat. Reserve ¼ cup (60ml) syrup. Add pecans to remaining syrup; simmer, for 5 minutes until syrup is thick and pecans are coated.

TIPS

You can swap pecans for walnuts. Cake can be made a day ahead; store in an airtight container. If you don't need to be dairy-free you can replace the dairy-free spread with butter and rice milk with cow's milk.

NUT FREE
GLUTEN FREE

**NUTRITIONAL
COUNT PER SERVING**
25.5g total fat
16.2g saturated fat
1926kJ (460 cal)
53g carbohydrate
4.4g protein
0.4g fibre

Mocha MERINGUE STACK

PREP + COOK TIME 1¾ HOURS (+ COOLING) SERVES 12

- 1 tablespoon instant coffee granules
- 1 teaspoon boiling water
- 8 egg whites
- 1 teaspoon cream of tartar
- 2 cups (440g) raw caster (superfine) sugar
- 1 tablespoon 100% corn (maize) cornflour (cornstarch)
- 2 teaspoons white vinegar
- 2 teaspoons gluten-free icing sugar (confectioners' sugar)

CHOCOLATE SAUCE

- 180g (5½ ounces) dark (semi-sweet) chocolate, chopped coarsely
- 30g (1 ounce) unsalted butter, chopped
- 1 cup (250ml) thickened (heavy) cream
- ¼ cup (40g) gluten-free icing sugar (confectioners' sugar)

COFFEE CREAM

- 1 tablespoon instant coffee granules
- 2 teaspoons boiling water
- 300ml thickened (heavy) cream
- ¼ cup (40g) gluten-free icing sugar (confectioners' sugar)
- 2 tablespoons coffee-flavoured liqueur
- 300ml thick (double) cream

1 Preheat oven to 120°C/250°F. Line three large oven trays with baking paper.

2 Stir coffee and the water in a small bowl until dissolved. Beat egg whites and cream of tartar in a large bowl with an electric mixer until soft peaks form. Gradually add caster sugar, beating until dissolved between additions. Beat in cornflour, vinegar and coffee mixture on low speed until just combined (overbeating at this stage will cause the meringue to deflate).

3 Drop large serving-spoon-sized amounts of meringue mixture (about ¼ cup) onto trays, 5cm (2 inches) apart; you should get about 24 meringues. Bake meringues for 1 hour or until dry to touch. Cool in oven with door ajar.

4 Make chocolate sauce, then coffee cream.

5 Spoon a little coffee cream onto a platter, arrange nine of the meringues on top. Spread the base of each remaining meringue with 2 tablespoons of coffee cream, stacking them into a pyramid shape. Drizzle stack with half the chocolate sauce, then dust with icing sugar. Serve stack immediately with coffee cream and the remaining sauce.

chocolate sauce Stir chocolate, butter and cream in a medium saucepan over low heat until just melted. Remove from heat; gradually whisk in sifted icing sugar. Cool to room temperature (about 20 minutes) until thickened.

coffee cream Stir coffee and the water in a small bowl until dissolved; refrigerate for 5 minutes. Beat thickened cream, icing sugar, liqueur and coffee mixture in a small bowl with an electric mixer until soft peaks form. Add thick cream; beat until soft peaks form.

TIPS

The meringues could take up to 1½ hours to cook, depending on the size of the oven. If you don't have enough space or shelves in your oven, make meringues in two batches. The meringues can be made 2 days ahead; store in an airtight container at room temperature. The sauce can be made several hours ahead; reheat until just warm before serving. Assemble meringue stack close to serving.

Elderflower & CRANBERRY ICE-POPS

PREP + COOK TIME 25 MINUTES (+ FREEZING) **MAKES** 24

- ⅓ cup (80ml) vodka
- ½ cup (125ml) elderflower cordial
- 2 tablespoons strained lime juice
- 1 cup (250ml) sparkling mineral water
- 2 tablespoons fresh mint leaves, sliced thinly
- 3 cups (750ml) cranberry juice

1 Combine vodka, cordial, lime juice and mineral water in a medium jug. Divide mixture between the moulds; sprinkle equally with mint. Wrap the mould completely in plastic wrap; insert the ice-block sticks into holes, piercing the plastic (the plastic wrap will help keep the sticks upright). Freeze for 6 hours or until mixture is frozen.

2 Pour cranberry juice over the vodka mint layer. Freeze for 2 hours or until juice is frozen.

3 Just before serving, rub the outside of the moulds with a hot kitchen cloth; gently remove ice-pops.

TIPS

You will need 24 x ¼-cup (60ml) ice-block moulds and 24 ice-block sticks. We used 60ml shot glasses and lollypop sticks to make our ice-pops. The ice-pops can be made several days ahead. For a non-alcoholic version, omit the vodka and add ⅓ cup extra mineral water.

Dairy free
NUT FREE
GLUTEN FREE
EGG FREE

**NUTRITIONAL
COUNT PER POP**
0g total fat
0g saturated fat
165kJ (39 cal)
7.9g carbohydrate
0g protein
0g fibre

NUT FREE
GLUTEN FREE
NUTRITIONAL COUNT PER SERVING
13.4g total fat
8.5g saturated fat
1133kJ (271 cal)
36.6g carbohydrate
2.2g protein
0.4g fibre

Lime & yoghurt cakes
WITH LIME SYRUP

PREP + COOK TIME 40 MINUTES MAKES 12

- 170g (5½ ounces) butter, softened
- ⅔ cup (150g) caster (superfine) sugar
- 1 tablespoon finely grated lime rind
- 2 eggs
- 1⅓ cups (180g) gluten-free self-raising flour
- 1 teaspon xanthan gum
- ⅔ cup (190g) greek-style yoghurt

LIME SYRUP

- 2 limes
- ½ cup (110g) caster (superfine) sugar
- ¾ cup (180ml) water

1 Preheat oven to 160°C/325°F. Grease 12-holes of a ⅓ cup (180ml) capacity mini kugelhopf pan.

2 Beat butter, sugar and rind in small bowl with an electric mixer until pale and fluffy. Beat in eggs, one at a time, until just combined. Transfer mixture to a large bowl; fold in sifted flour, gum and yoghurt, in two batches. Spoon mixture into holes; smooth surface.

3 Bake cakes for 25 minutes or until a skewer inserted into the centre comes out clean. Stand cakes in pans for 5 minutes before turning onto a wire rack placed over an oven tray.

4 Meanwhile, make lime syrup.

5 Pour hot syrup evenly over hot cakes. Serve cakes warm with extra yoghurt, if you like.

lime syrup Peel rind from limes into 1cm (½-inch) wide strips; place in a small saucepan, cover with water. Bring to the boil; drain. Repeat 4 more times. Meanwhile, squeeze limes; you will need ¼ cup (60ml) juice. Return rind to pan with sugar, the water and juice; stir, over medium heat, until sugar dissolved. Simmer, uncovered, for 15 minutes or until syrup has thickened.

TIPS

These cakes are best served warm on the day you make them. Cakes can be reheated in the microwave on HIGH (100%) in 10-second bursts until heated through.

Individual boiled puddings
WITH ORANGE CUSTARD

PREP + COOK TIME 2½ HOURS MAKES 6

- 1kg (2 pounds) mixed fruit
- 1 large green apple (200g), grated coarsely
- ½ cup (125ml) grand marnier (orange-flavoured liqueur)
- 1 tablespoon finely grated orange rind
- 2 teaspoons mixed spice
- 2 teaspoons ground cinnamon
- 125g (4 ounces) butter, softened
- ½ cup (110g) firmly packed dark brown sugar
- 2 eggs
- 2 cups (140g) stale gluten-free white breadcrumbs
- ½ cup (75g) tapioca flour
- 1 cup (135g) gluten-free plain (all-purpose) flour
- 6 x 35cm (14-inch) square unbleached calico

ORANGE CUSTARD

- 1½ cups (375ml) vanilla custard
- 2 tablespoons grand marnier (orange-flavoured liqueur)

1 Combine mixed fruit, apple, grand marnier, rind, mixed spice and cinnamon in a large bowl. Cover with plastic wrap; stand at room temperature overnight.

2 Beat butter and sugar in a small bowl with an electric mixer until pale. Beat in eggs, one at a time. Stir egg mixture into fruit mixture. Add breadcrumbs and combined sifted flours; stir to combine.

3 Fill a boiler three quarters full of hot water, cover with a tight fitting lid; bring to the boil. Have ready 1 metre (3 feet) of kitchen string, plus extra flour. Wearing thick rubber gloves and using tongs, dip pudding cloths, one at a time, into boiling water; boil 1 minute, then remove. Squeeze excess water from cloth. Spread hot cloths on bench; rub 2 tablespoons of the extra flour into centre of each cloth to cover an area about 20m (8 inches) in diameter, leaving flour a little thicker in centre of cloth where "skin" on the pudding needs to be thickest. Divide pudding mixture equally among cloths; placing in centre of each cloth. Gather cloths around mixture, avoiding any deep pleats; pat into round shapes. Tie cloths tightly with string, as close to mixture as possible Tie loops in string. Lower three puddings into boiling water. Cover; boil 2 hours, replenishing with boiling water as necessary to maintain water level.

4 Lift puddings from water, one at a time, using wooden spoons through string loops. Do not put pudding on bench; suspend from spoon by placing over rungs of upturned stool or wedging the spoon in a drawer. Twist ends of cloth around string to avoid them touching pudding; hang 10 minutes. Repeat with remaining puddings.

5 Place puddings on board; cut string, carefully peel back cloth. Turn puddings onto plate, then carefully peel cloth away completely. Stand 20 minutes or until skin darkens and pudding becomes firm.

6 Make orange custard. Serve puddings with custard.

orange custard Combine ingredients in a small bowl.

tips This recipe makes six generous single serve puddings. For a non-alcoholic pudding, use orange juice instead of the liqueur. You will need six 35cm (14-inch) square pudding cloths. Puddings can be cooked in two boilers or in batches; mixture will keep at room temperature for several hours. If you are giving puddings as gifts, hang the puddings in their cloths until cold; they can be stored, in the fridge, for up to 2 months, or frozen for up to 12 months. To reheat puddings, lower clothed puddings into boiling water and boil, for about 1 hour following steps 4 and 5. To reheat in microwave, cover unclothed pudding with plastic wrap and microwave on MEDIUM (55%) for about 5 minutes or until hot.

NUT FREE
GLUTEN FREE

NUTRITIONAL COUNT PER PUDDING
23.7g total fat
13.6g saturated fat
4468kJ (1067 cal)
191.8g carbohydrate
10.8g protein
11.4g fibre

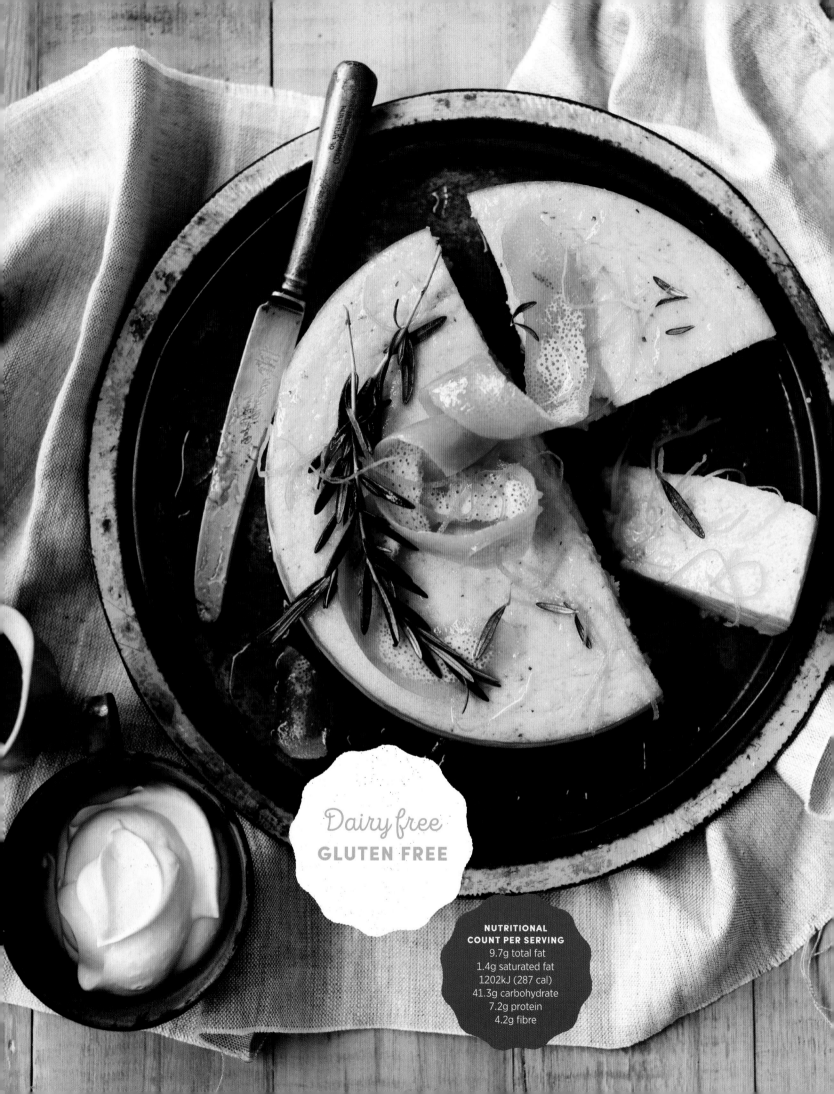

Dairy free
GLUTEN FREE

**NUTRITIONAL
COUNT PER SERVING**
9.7g total fat
1.4g saturated fat
1202kJ (287 cal)
41.3g carbohydrate
7.2g protein
4.2g fibre

Whole orange semolina cake
WITH ROSEMARY SYRUP

PREP + COOK TIME 2 HOURS 40 MINUTES (+ STANDING) **SERVES** 12

- 2 large oranges (600g)
- 1 teaspoon gluten-free baking powder
- 6 eggs
- 1 cup (220g) caster (superfine) sugar
- 1 cup (150g) fine semolina
- 1¼ cups (150g) ground almonds
- 1½ teaspoons finely chopped fresh rosemary leaves

ROSEMARY SYRUP
- 2 large oranges (600g)
- ½ cup (110g) caster (superfine) sugar
- ½ cup (125ml) water
- 1½ tablespoons lemon juice
- 2 tablespoons orange-flavoured liqueur
- 2 x 8cm (3¼-inch) sprigs fresh rosemary

1 Place whole unpeeled oranges in a medium saucepan over high heat, cover with cold water; bring to the boil. Boil, covered, 1½ hours or until oranges are tender; drain. Cool.

2 Preheat oven to 180°C/350°F. Grease a deep 22cm (9-inch) round cake pan; line the base and side with baking paper.

3 Trim and discard ends from oranges. Halve oranges; discard seeds. Process orange, including rind, with baking powder until mixture is pulpy. Transfer to a large bowl.

4 Process eggs and sugar for 5 minutes or until thick and creamy. Stir egg mixture into orange mixture. Fold in semolina, ground almonds and rosemary. Spread mixture into pan.

5 Bake cake for 1 hour or until a skewer inserted into the centre comes out clean. Stand cake in pan for 45 minutes before turning, top-side up, onto a cake plate.

6 Make rosemary syrup.

7 Spoon hot syrup over warm cake. Serve cake warm or at room temperature.

rosemary syrup Remove rind from 1 orange with a zester, into thin strips. Using a vegetable peeler, peel a long continuous strip of rind from remaining orange. Place sugar, the water and juice in a small saucepan over low heat; stir, without boiling, until sugar dissolves. Add long strip of rind, bring to the boil; boil for 5 minutes or until syrup thickens. Remove from heat; stir in liqueur, rosemary and thin strips of rind.

TIPS

If you don't have a zester, simply peel the rind into wide strips with a vegetable peeler, then cut them into thin strips. You could vary the flavourings in the syrup by adding either a cinnamon stick or a split vanilla bean instead of the rosemary. The cake is best made on day of serving.

Gluten-free DOUGHNUTS

PREP + COOK TIME 1½ HOURS (+ STANDING) **MAKES** 16

- 3 cups (405g) gluten-free plain (all-purpose) flour
- ½ cup (75g) 100% corn (maize) cornflour (cornstarch)
- ½ cup (90g) white rice flour
- ½ cup (65g) gluten-free self-raising flour
- 2 teaspoons (7g) dried yeast
- ¼ cup (55g) caster (superfine) sugar
- 3 eggs
- 185g (6 ounces) butter, melted
- 1 teaspoon vanilla essence
- 1½ cups (375ml) milk
- cooking oil spray
- vegetable oil, for deep frying
- 1 teaspoon ground cinnamon
- 1 tablespoon caster (superfine) sugar, extra

1 Combine sifted flours, yeast and sugar in a large bowl.

2 Beat eggs, butter, vanilla and 1 cup (250ml) of milk in a large bowl of electric mixer, on medium speed for 3 minutes. Add remaining milk and the flour mixture, 1 cup at a time, beating until combined and smooth.

3 Spoon mixture into a large piping bag fitted with a plain 2cm (¾-inch) piping tube.

4 Pipe mixture onto baking-paper-lined oven trays, into 7cm (2¾-inch) circles. Spray doughnuts with cooking oil spray. Cover with plastic wrap; stand in a warm place for 40 minutes or until doubled in size.

5 Heat oil in a large, deep frying pan to 180°C/350°F. Using a pair of scissors; cut the baking paper into squares around the doughnuts. Pick up the doughnuts with baking paper and gently place, one at a time, upside-down into the hot oil (baking paper will fall off as the doughnut cooks, remove baking paper from oil with tongs). Cook for 3 minutes on each side or until golden brown. Remove from oil using a slotted spoon; drain on paper towel.

6 Toss hot doughnuts in combined cinnamon and extra sugar; serve immediately.

TIPS

Use a deep-frying thermometer to get an accurate temperature when frying. Doughnuts are best eaten just after they are cooked. They will firm on standing, so microwave on HIGH (100%) in 10-second burst until warm and soft.

**NUTRITIONAL
COUNT PER
DOUGHNUT**
15.9g total fat
7.7g saturated fat
1317kJ (315 cal)
39.8g carbohydrate
3.4g protein
0.2g fibre

4 ways with DOUGHNUTS

NUT FREE
GLUTEN FREE

NUTRITIONAL COUNT PER DOUGHNUT
16.8g total fat
8.5g saturated fat
1492kJ (357 cal)
47.7g carbohydrate
4.4g protein
0.1g fibre

NUTRITIONAL COUNT PER DOUGHNUT
13.6 g total fat
6.5g saturated fat
1384kJ (331 cal)
50g carbohydrate
2.9g protein
0.1g fibre

CUSTARD-FILLED DOUGHNUTS

PREP + COOK TIME 1½ HOURS (+ STANDING)
MAKES 16

Follow the gluten-free doughnuts recipe on page 230 to the end of step 3. Holding the piping bag directly over top of the baking-paper-lined oven tray, squeeze until batter makes a 5cm (2-in) round; repeat to make 16 in total. Using a wet fingertip, pat down any peaks on top. Continue following recipe to the end of step 5, cooking for an extra 5 minutes. Toss hot doughnuts in ½ cup (80g) sifted gluten-free icing sugar (confectioners' sugar), before cooling. Fill a large piping bag fitted with a 1cm (½-in) plain piping tube with 1⅔ cups (410ml) gluten-free double thick French vanilla custard. Pierce the top of each doughnut with the piping tube and gently pipe custard directly into the doughnut until it starts to squeeze out the top.

LEMON-GLAZED DOUGHNUTS

PREP + COOK TIME 1½ HOURS (+ STANDING)
MAKES 16

Follow the gluten-free doughnuts recipe on page 230 to the end of step 5. Sift 2 cups (320g) gluten-free icing sugar (confectioners' sugar) into a medium bowl. Add ¼ cup (60ml) lemon juice; stir until smooth. Dip cooled doughnuts upside-down into lemon glaze. Transfer to a wire rack; stand until set.

**NUTRITIONAL
COUNT PER
DOUGHNUT**
22.2g total fat
11.7g saturated fat
1935kJ (463 cal)
63.4g carbohydrate
3.8g protein
0.2g fibre

**NUTRITIONAL
COUNT PER
DOUGHNUT**
16g total fat
7.7g saturated fat
1789kJ (428 cal)
67.5g carbohydrate
3.5g protein
0.1g fibre

JAM-FILLED DOUGHNUTS

**PREP + COOK TIME 1½ HOURS (+ STANDING)
MAKES 16**

Follow the gluten-free doughnuts recipe on page 230 to the end of step 3. Holding the piping bag directly over top of the baking-paper-lined oven tray, squeeze until batter makes a 6cm (2½-in) round; repeat to make 16 in total. Continue following recipe to the end of step 5, cooking for an extra 5 minutes. Toss hot doughnuts in ½ cup (110g) caster (superfine) sugar before cooling slightly. Fill a large piping bag fitted with a 1cm (½-in) plain piping tube with 1⅔ cups (540g) sieved raspberry jam. Pierce the top of each doughnut with the piping tube and gently pipe jam directly into the doughnut until it starts to squeeze out the top.

CHOCOLATE-GLAZED DOUGHNUTS

**PREP + COOK TIME 1½ HOURS (+ STANDING)
MAKES 16**

Follow the gluten-free doughnuts recipe on page 230 to the end of step 5. Melt 80g (2½oz) butter and 120g (4oz) dark chocolate in a small pan over low heat, stirring, for 3 minutes or until smooth. Stir in 2 cups (320g) gluten-free icing sugar (confectioners' sugar) and approximately ⅓ cup (80ml) water to make a smooth runny glaze. Cool glaze for 5 minutes or until thickened slightly. Dip warm doughnuts upside-down into chocolate glaze. Transfer to a wire rack; stand until set.

GLOSSARY

agave syrup a sweetener commercially produced from the agave plant in South Africa and Mexico. It is sweeter than sugar, though less viscous, so it dissolves quickly. Agave syrup is sold in light, amber, dark, and raw varieties.

almonds

blanched brown skins removed.

flaked paper-thin slices.

ground also called almond meal.

baking paper also called baking parchment or parchment paper; a silicone-coated paper primarily used to line baking pans and oven trays so cooked food doesn't stick.

baking powder, gluten-free a raising agent; readily available from supermarkets.

beans

cannellini small white bean similar to great northern, navy and haricot beans, which can be substituted for each other. Available dried or canned.

snake long (about 40cm/16 inches), thin, round, fresh green bean; Asian in origin with a taste similar to green beans.

bicarbonate of soda (baking soda) used as a leavening agent in baking.

butter use salted or unsalted butter; 125g is equal to one stick (4 ounces) of butter.

capsicum (bell pepper) available in red, green, yellow, orange and purplish-black. Discard seeds and membranes before use.

cardamom a spice native to India and used extensively in its cuisine; available in pod, seed or ground form. Has a distinctive aromatic, sweetly rich flavour.

celeriac (celery root) tuberous root with knobbly brown skin, white flesh and a celery-like flavour. Keep peeled celeriac in acidulated water to stop it discolouring. It can be grated and eaten raw in salads; used in soups and stews; boiled and mashed like potatoes; or sliced thinly and deep-fried as chips.

cheese

fetta Greek in origin; a crumbly textured goat- or sheep-milk cheese with a sharp, salty taste.

fetta, persian a soft, creamy fetta marinated in a blend of olive oil, garlic, herbs and spices; available from most major supermarkets.

haloumi a Greek Cypriot cheese with a semi-firm, spongy texture and very salty sweet flavour. Ripened and stored in salted whey; best grilled or fried, it holds its shape well on being heated. Eat while still warm as it becomes tough and rubbery on cooling.

mozzarella a soft, spun-curd cheese. It has a low melting point and an elastic texture when heated and is used to add texture rather than flavour.

parmesan also called parmigiano; is a hard, grainy cow-milk cheese originating in Italy.

ricotta a soft, sweet, moist, white cow-milk cheese with a low fat content and a slightly grainy texture. The name roughly translates as 'cooked again' and refers to ricotta's manufacture from a whey that is itself a by-product of other cheese making.

chervil mildly fennel-flavoured member of the parsley family with curly dark-green leaves. Available fresh and dried but, like all herbs, is best used fresh; like coriander and parsley, its delicate flavour diminishes the longer it's cooked.

chia seeds contain protein, all the essential amino acids and a wealth of vitamins, minerals and antioxidants, as well as being fibre-rich.

chickpeas (garbanzo beans) also called hummus or channa; an irregularly round, sandy-coloured legume. Available canned or dried (soak in cold water before use).

chilli generally, the smaller the chilli, the hotter it is. Use rubber gloves when seeding and chopping fresh chillies as they can burn your skin. Removing seeds and membranes lessens the heat level.

chocolate

choc bits also called chocolate chips and chocolate morsels; available in dark, milk, white and caramel. They hold their shape in baking and are ideal for decorating.

dairy-free dark buy a high-quality dark chocolate, which should only contain cocoa butter, cocoa liquor, lecithin (usually soy-based) and sugar. It should not contain any milk products; always check the ingredient label.

dark (semi-sweet) made of a high percentage of cocoa liquor and cocoa butter, and little added sugar. It is ideal for desserts and cakes.

Melts discs of compound chocolate ideal for melting and moulding.

white contains no cocoa solids but derives its sweet flavour from cocoa butter. Very sensitive to heat so be careful if melting.

cinnamon available in pieces (called sticks or quills) and ground into powder; one of the world's most common spices.

cocoa powder or cocoa; dried, unsweetened, roasted then ground cocoa beans (cacao seeds).

dutch-processed is treated with an alkali to neutralize its acids. It has a reddish-brown colour, mild flavour, and is easy to dissolve in liquids.

coconut

desiccated concentrated, unsweetened, dried and finely shredded coconut flesh.

flaked dried, flaked, coconut flesh.

milk not the liquid inside (coconut water), but the diluted liquid from the second pressing of the white flesh of a mature coconut (the first pressing produces coconut cream). Available in cans and cartons at most supermarkets.

oil is extracted from the coconut flesh, so you don't get any of the fibre, protein or carbohydrates present in the whole coconut. The best quality is virgin coconut oil, which is the oil pressed from the dried coconut flesh, and doesn't include the use of solvents or other refining processes.

shredded unsweetened thin strips of dried coconut flesh.

sugar is not made from coconuts, but the sap of the blossoms of the coconut palm tree. The refined sap looks a little like raw or light brown sugar, and has a similar caramel flavour. It also has the same amount of kilojoules as regular white (granulated) sugar.

cornflour (cornstarch) thickening agent available in two forms: 100% corn (maize), which is gluten free, and a wheaten cornflour (made from wheat) which is not.

cream

pouring also called pure or fresh cream. Has no additives and contains a minimum fat content of 35%.

thickened (heavy) a whipping cream that contains a thickener; it has a minimum fat content of 35%.

cream of tartar the acid ingredient in baking powder; added to confectionery mixtures to help prevent sugar from crystallising. Keeps frostings creamy and improves volume when beating egg whites.

crème fraîche mature fermented cream with a slightly tangy, nutty flavour and velvety texture. Used in savoury and sweet dishes. Minimum fat content 35%.

cumin a spice also called zeera or comino; has a spicy, nutty flavour.

fish sauce also called nam pla or nuoc nam; made from pulverised salted fermented fish, most often anchovies. Has a pungent smell and strong taste; use sparingly.

flour

brown rice retains the outer bran layer of the rice grain. Contains no gluten. It has a slightly chewy texture and nut-like flavour.

buckwheat not actually a form of wheat, but a herb in the same plant family as rhubarb; it is gluten-free. Has a strong nutty taste.

chickpea (besan) also called gram; made from ground chickpeas so is gluten-free and high in protein.

gluten-free plain (all-purpose) a blend of gluten-free flours and starches (may include corn, potato, tapioca, chickpea and rice).

gluten-free self-raising made similarly to gluten-free plain flour, but with the addition of gluten-free bicarbonate of soda (baking soda).

potato made from cooked, dehydrated and ground potato; not to be confused with potato starch which is made from potato starch only. Potato flour has a strong potato flavour and is a heavy flour so a little goes a long way.

rice very fine, almost powdery, gluten-free flour; made from ground white rice.

tapioca made from the root of the cassava plant; a soft, fine, light white flour.

gelatine we used powdered gelatine. It is also available in sheet form, known as leaf gelatine.

ginger, fresh also called green or root ginger; thick gnarled root of a tropical plant.

gluten is a combination of two proteins found in wheat (including spelt), rye, barley and oats. When liquid is added to the flour, these two proteins bind to become gluten. Gluten gives elasticity to dough, helping it rise and keep its shape; it also gives the final product a chewy texture.

golden syrup a by-product of refined sugarcane; pure maple syrup or honey can be substituted.

horseradish cream a paste of grated horseradish, mustard seeds, oil and sugar. Available from supermarkets.

kaffir lime leaves sold fresh, dried or frozen; looks like two glossy dark green leaves joined end to end, forming a rounded hourglass shape. Dried leaves are less potent, so double the number called for in a recipe if you substitute them for fresh. A strip of fresh lime peel may be substituted for each leaf.

lemon grass also known as takrai, serai or serah. A tall, clumping, lemon-smelling and tasting, sharp-edged aromatic tropical grass; the white lower part of the stem is used, finely chopped, in many South-East Asian dishes. Can be found fresh, dried, powdered and frozen, in supermarkets, greengrocers and Asian food shops.

maple syrup, pure a thin syrup distilled from the sap of the maple tree. Maple-flavoured syrup or pancake syrup is not an adequate substitute for the real thing.

mixed spice a blend of ground spices usually cinnamon, allspice and nutmeg.

mushrooms

enoki clumps of long, spaghetti-like stems with tiny, snowy white caps.

oyster also called abalone; grey-white mushrooms shaped like a fan. Prized for their smooth texture and subtle, oyster-like flavour. Also available pink.

shiitake, fresh also known as chinese black, forest or golden oak mushrooms; although cultivated, they are large and meaty and have the earthiness and taste of wild mushrooms.

swiss brown also called roman or cremini. Light to dark brown mushrooms with full-bodied flavour; suited for use in casseroles or being stuffed and baked.

norbu (monk fruit sugar) monk fruit is a subtropical melon that contains a group of sweet tasting antioxidant compounds. Used as an alternative to cane sugar, as it has 96% fewer kilojoules and will not affect blood glucose or insulin levels.

oil

coconut see coconut

cooking spray we use a cholesterol-free cooking spray made from canola oil, unless stated otherwise.

olive made from ripened olives. Extra virgin and virgin are the best, while extra light or light refers to taste not fat levels.

onion, green (scallion) also called (incorrectly) shallot; an immature onion picked before the bulb has formed, with a long, bright green edible stalk.

orange blossom water concentrated flavouring made from orange blossoms.

pastry, gluten-free made from a blend of gluten-free flours and starches (may include corn, rice, tapioca, potato starch, pea) and binding and raising agents. Available in health-food stores, and in the health-food section of most supermarkets.

pepitas (pumpkin seeds) are the pale green kernels of dried pumpkin seeds.

polenta also called cornmeal; a flourlike cereal made of dried corn (maize) sold ground in different textures.

pomegranate dark-red, leathery-skinned fruit about the size of an orange filled with hundreds of seeds, each wrapped in an edible lucent-crimson pulp with a unique tangy sweet-sour flavour.

quinoa pronounced keen-wa; it is the seed of a leafy plant similar to spinach. It has a delicate, slightly nutty taste and chewy texture.

flakes the quinoa grains have been rolled and flattened.

rice cereal, gluten-free baby made from ground rice and sunflower oil; always check the packaging as some may also contain traces of wheat, milk and soy.

rice flakes is a dehusked rice which is flattened into flat light dry flakes. These flakes swell when added to liquid. Easily digestible form of rice.

roasting/toasting nuts and dried coconut can be roasted in the oven to restore their fresh flavour and release their aromatic essential oils. Spread evenly on an oven tray; roast in a 180°C oven about 5 minutes. Pine nuts, sesame seeds and desiccated coconut toast more evenly if stirred over low heat in a heavy-based frying pan.

rocket (arugula) a peppery-tasting green leaf. Baby rocket leaves, also called wild rocket, are both smaller and less peppery.

silver beet mistakenly called spinach; a member of the beet family grown for its tasty green leaves and celery-like stems. Best cooked rather than eaten raw.

spinach also known as english spinach. Its thick, soft oval leaves and green stems are both edible. Baby spinach is also available.

sugar

brown a very soft, fine granulated sugar retaining molasses for its characteristic colour and flavour.

caster (superfine) finely granulated table sugar.

gluten-free icing (confectioners') also called powdered sugar; pulverised granulated sugar crushed together with a small amount of corn (maize) cornflour (cornstarch).

pure icing (confectioners') also called powdered sugar; contains no cornflour.

tahini is a sesame seed paste available from Middle-Eastern food stores and some supermarkets.

tamari sauce a thick, dark soy sauce made mainly from soy beans and without the wheat used in standard soy sauce.

tofutti a tofu-based dairy-free cream cheese substitute, available in the refrigerated section of health food stores and major supermarkets.

tomato, canned peeled tomatoes in natural juices; available whole, crushed, chopped or diced. Use undrained.

turmeric a member of the ginger family; must be grated or pounded to release

its acrid aroma and pungent flavour. Known for the golden colour it imparts, fresh turmeric can be substituted with the more commonly found dried powder.

vanilla

bean dried, long, thin pod from a tropical golden orchid; the minuscule black seeds inside the bean impart a luscious flavour in baking and desserts.

extract made by extracting the flavour from the vanilla bean pod; the pods are soaked, usually in alcohol, to capture the authentic flavour.

paste made from vanilla beans and contains real seeds. Is highly concentrated: 1 teaspoon replaces a whole bean. Found in most supermarkets in the baking section.

watercress one of the cress family, a large group of peppery greens. Highly perishable, it must be used as soon as possible after purchase.

xanthan gum is a thickening agent produced by fermentation of, usually, corn sugar. When buying xanthan gum, ensure the packet states 'made from fermented corn sugar'. Found in the health-food section in larger supermarkets.

yoghurt

greek-style plain yoghurt strained in a cloth (traditionally muslin) to remove the whey and to give it a creamy consistency.

soy an alternative to dairy yoghurt; usually an excellent source of calcium.

zucchini also called courgette.

Mini Gingerbread House Templates
(recipe page 214)

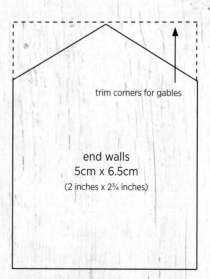

trim corners for gables

roof
6cm x 3.5cm
(2½ inches x 1½ inches)

side walls
5cm x 5cm
(2 inches x 2 inches)

end walls
5cm x 6.5cm
(2 inches x 2¾ inches)

CONVERSION CHART

MEASURES

One Australian metric measuring cup holds approximately 250ml; one Australian metric tablespoon holds 20ml; one Australian metric teaspoon holds 5ml.

The difference between one country's measuring cups and another's is within a two- or three-teaspoon variance, and will not affect your cooking results. North America, New Zealand and the United Kingdom use a 15ml tablespoon. All cup and spoon measurements are level. The most accurate way of measuring dry ingredients is to weigh them. When measuring liquids, use a clear glass or plastic jug with the metric markings.

We use large eggs with an average weight of 60g.

DRY MEASURES

metric	imperial
15g	½oz
30g	1oz
60g	2oz
90g	3oz
125g	4oz (¼lb)
155g	5oz
185g	6oz
220g	7oz
250g	8oz (½lb)
280g	9oz
315g	10oz
345g	11oz
375g	12oz (¾lb)
410g	13oz
440g	14oz
470g	15oz
500g	16oz (1lb)
750g	24oz (1½lb)
1kg	32oz (2lb)

LIQUID MEASURES

metric	imperial
30ml	1 fluid oz
60ml	2 fluid oz
100ml	3 fluid oz
125ml	4 fluid oz
150ml	5 fluid oz
190ml	6 fluid oz
250ml	8 fluid oz
300ml	10 fluid oz
500ml	16 fluid oz
600ml	20 fluid oz
1000ml (1 litre)	1¾ pints

LENGTH MEASURES

metric	imperial
3mm	⅛in
6mm	¼in
1cm	½in
2cm	¾in
2.5cm	1in
5cm	2in
6cm	2½in
8cm	3in
10cm	4in
13cm	5in
15cm	6in
18cm	7in
20cm	8in
22cm	9in
25cm	10in
28cm	11in
30cm	12in (1ft)

OVEN TEMPERATURES

The oven temperatures in this book are for conventional ovens; if you have a fan-forced oven, decrease the temperature by 10-20 degrees.

	°C (Celsius)	°F (Fahrenheit)
Very slow	120	250
Slow	150	300
Moderately slow	160	325
Moderate	180	350
Moderately hot	200	400
Hot	220	425
Very hot	240	475

THE IMPERIAL MEASUREMENTS USED IN THESE RECIPES ARE APPROXIMATE ONLY. MEASUREMENTS FOR CAKE PANS ARE APPROXIMATE ONLY. USING SAME-SHAPED CAKE PANS OF A SIMILAR SIZE SHOULD NOT AFFECT THE OUTCOME OF YOUR BAKING. WE MEASURE THE INSIDE TOP OF THE CAKE PAN TO DETERMINE SIZES.

INDEX